Welsh Words

Am restr gyflawn o lyfrau'r Lolfa, hwyliwch i mewn i'n gwefan **www.ylolfa.com** lle gallwch chwilio ac archebu ar-lein.

For a full list of Lolfa publications, go to our website **www.ylolfa.com** where you may browse and order online.

STEVE MORRIS & PAUL MEARA

Welsh Words

Core vocabulary with phrases

Geirfa Graidd: Lefel Mynediad

South Wales

Argraffiad cyntaf: 2014

Dylunio: Robat Gruffudd/Y Lolfa

Rhif Llyfr Rhyngwladol: 978-1-84771-981-2

Cyhoeddwyd ac argraffwyd yng Nghymru
ar bapur o goedwigoedd cynaladwy gan
Y Lolfa Cyf., Talybont, Ceredigion SY24 5HE
gwefan www.ylolfa.com
e-bost ylolfa@ylolfa.com
ffôn 01970 832 304
ffacs 832 782

Diolch / Thanks

Mae'r eirfa graidd yn y llyfr hwn yn seiliedig ar brosiect ymchwil gan yr awduron ym Mhrifysgol Abertawe. Hoffem ddiolch i'r chwe deg o diwtoriaid a gyfrannodd (yn gyson, dros nifer o fisoedd) i'r ymchwil tu ôl i'r eirfa graidd. Oni bai am eich parodrwydd chi i ymgymryd â'r gwaith ychwanegol hwn, fyddai'r eirfa graidd ddim gyda ni.

Hoffem ddiolch i Mark Stonelake ac yn arbennig i Elwyn Hughes am eu sylwadau gwerthfawr ac adeiladol (yn enwedig, yn achos Elwyn, gyda / efo fersiwn y gogledd) ac i aelodau gweithgor arholiadau Mynediad a Sylfaen CBAC ac i Emyr Davies a Janette Jones, CBAC.

Ac yn olaf, diolch i Meleri Wyn James a staff y Lolfa am eu gwaith manwl a'u cyngor defnyddiol wrth fynd â'r gwaith yma i'r wasg.

The core vocabulary in this book is based on a research project by the authors at Swansea University. We would like to thank the sixty tutors who contributed (regularly, over a number of months) to the research behind this core vocabulary. Were it not for your willingness to undertake this additional work, we wouldn't have the core vocabulary.

We would like to thank Mark Stonelake and in particular Elwyn Hughes for their valuable and constructive comments (especially in Elwyn's case with the north Wales version) and the members of the WJEC Mynediad and Sylfaen examinations committee and Emyr Davies and Janette Jones, at the WJEC.

And finally, thanks to Meleri Wyn James and the staff at y Lolfa for their detailed work and their useful advice in getting this work to press.

Steve Morris & Paul Meara

HOW TO GET THE MOST OUT OF THIS BOOK

What is *Geirfa Graidd*?

The first thing to remember above all else is that this is not an exhaustive list of all the vocabulary you will ever need to be able to cope with Mynediad level Welsh for Adults! This is **'Geirfa Graidd'** – a **core vocabulary**. In other words, the items listed here are all those that our work has shown are necessary to know in order to achieve Mynediad level, that is the words you would be expected to know (and to be able to use) by the end of a Mynediad level course.

What does that mean?

It means that:

- Public Welsh for Adults exams at this level would assume you know these items and would be able to use them when you speak, write and read Welsh. Any items **not** in the **Geirfa Graidd** would normally be explained or an English translation given in brackets afterwards.
- Learning and teaching materials aimed at Mynediad level will include these items and this is the core vocabulary for inclusion in them. However, every course or learning resource will inevitably include far more items than just the **Geirfa Graidd**. The important thing to remember is that the **Geirfa Graidd: Mynediad** includes all the items you **need** to know to achieve Mynediad level, but as well as these there will be many other items of vocabulary which you will need and will be specific to you and your circumstances. Knowing these items, and being able to talk about things or people which mean a lot to you, is every bit as important as knowing the **Geirfa Graidd**: it's just that

the **Geirfa Graidd** is vocabulary which is common to all learners at this level.

OK – so what's in the book?

Every item of vocabulary which forms the **Geirfa Graidd: Mynediad** is listed in this book. As well as every item of vocabulary, you will also find:

- A translation of the item into English.
- Notes to tell you if there is a more standard alternative which you might come across as well as, sometimes, whether the item causes a mutation.
- Some verbs are usually followed by certain prepositions. If this is the case, this will be also be shown. Try to remember any connections like these and memorise them together.
- When the item is a noun, you will also be given (i) the gender and (ii) the plural form, in most cases.
- In order for you to see **how** the item is used, each one includes an example of the item in context i.e. a chance for you to see it in use. These are followed by an English translation just to make the meaning and context completely clear. The examples all use patterns which should be familiar to learners towards the end of Mynediad level courses.
- Sometimes, other phrases and idioms are formed with the main item of vocabulary. These are listed under the main element e.g. *beic* [= bike] with *mynd ar gefn beic* [= to ride a bike] listed underneath it (not under 'M').

You can think of it as a mini dictionary of vocabulary which is designed specifically for adult learners of Welsh at Mynediad level. Use it to help you learn this vocabulary. To assist you further with that task, at the end of the book, Professor Paul Meara (an international expert in vocabulary acquisition and processing), has included his top ten tips on **how** to learn vocabulary. As he says, 'you might find that the techniques don't all work for you...' and don't worry: this is normal! Every one of us learns in different ways and what works for one learner won't necessarily work for another. Experiment, and when you find a technique or techniques which help you, then concentrate on them. Some of these techniques may become more useful when you progress beyond Mynediad level, so read through them often and give them a go!

What do the abbreviations mean?

Throughout the book, we have used a few abbreviations to save space and give you more information about different items. Here's an explanation of what they mean:

[eb]	enw benywaidd	*[feminine noun]*
[eg]	enw gwrywaidd	*[masculine noun]*
[ell]	enw lluosog	*[plural noun]*

This will be helpful for you to know when it comes to actually using these items. For example, if you see **eb** which tells you that a noun is a *feminine noun*, you will also know that (i) it takes a soft mutation after '**y** / **yr** / '**r**' (ii) an adjective following it will take the soft mutation and (iii) you will need the feminine versions of numbers (**dwy** / **tair** / **pedair**) instead of the masculine ones.

SW	South Wales i.e. an alternative which is normally only used in south Wales
+ Treiglad Meddal	followed by a Soft Mutation
+ Treiglad Llaes	followed by an Aspirate Mutation

+ Treiglad Trwynol   followed by a Nasal Mutation

Why do some words have an asterisk * by the side of them?

A few of the items in the **Geirfa Graidd** have an asterisk by the side of them. This is to show you that they are items you should **understand** (for example, they might be items involved in classroom work e.g. **cyfieithu** – translate), but that you would not be expected to use at this level of learning Welsh.

What's not included...

- Forms of verbs with endings added. The main **berfenw** (verb-noun) is included but forms with endings are not included in the list. For example, **mynd** (*to go*) is listed but **es i** (*I went*) is not. Similarly, **bod** (*to be*) is there but **roeddwn i** (*I was*) is not.

- Names of towns, cities, counties etc. This does not apply to names of countries where relevant.

- A very small number of untranslatable, pattern / grammar items.

It looks like there are some English words in the list! Why have they been included?

They might look like English words – and indeed there are many borrowings from English in Welsh. However, if they are words which are used frequently and have become accepted into contemporary spoken Welsh e.g. **pensil, lemon, ffilm**, then you need to know:

(i) that this is how to say *'pencil'*, *'lemon'* and *'film'* in Welsh

(ii) whether they are masculine or feminine (so that you know whether to use 'dau ffilm' or 'dwy ffilm' and whether you say 'ffilm da' or 'ffilm dda') and

(iii) what the plural form is.

And finally...

Mastering vocabulary appropriate to the level at which you
are learning is vital to success in any language learning.
Use this book to help you to learn and absorb the core
vocabulary you need to succeed at Mynediad level in Welsh.
Don't forget that these are the **core** words you'll need at this
level. You'll also need to learn many others so that you can
talk confidently at Mynediad level about everything that is
important and relevant in your own particular lives. These
will be specific to you and you should compile a list of them
to keep handy with this book. Together they will arm you
with the vocabulary you will need to reach Mynediad level
and move on beyond it. Mwynhewch!

Steve Morris & Paul Meara
Swansea, July 2014

A

A / Ac	*And*
	*Aeth Jack **a** Jill i weld y gêm.*
	***Jack and** Jill went to see the game.*
	*Aeth Siân **ac** Ifan i weld y gêm.*
	***Siân and** Ifan went to see the game.*
	*[Followed by **Treiglad Llaes** in formal speech]*
	*Mae'r caffi'n gwerthu te **a ch**offi.*
	***The café sells tea and** coffee.*
Actor *[eg]*	*Actor*
> actorion	
Actores *[eb]*	*Actress*
> actoresau	*Roedd Richard Burton yn **actor** enwog.*
	Richard Burton was a famous actor.
	*Roedd Elizabeth Taylor yn **actores** enwog.*
	Elizabeth Taylor was a famous actress.
Achos	*Because*
	*Agorais i'r ffenest **achos** roedd hi'n dwym yn y stafell.*
	*I opened the window **because** it was hot in the room.*
Adeiladu	*To build*
	*Bydd Bob yn helpu i **adeiladu**'r tŷ newydd.*
	Bob will help build the new house.
Adeiladwr *[eg]*	*Builder*
> adeiladwyr	*Bydd Bob yr **adeiladwr** yn gweithio ar y tŷ newydd.*
	***Bob the builder** will be working on the new house*

Adolygu
To revise
Cyn yr arholiad, roedd pawb yn y dosbarth yn **adolygu** *gyda'r tiwtor.*
Before the exam, everyone in the class was **revising** *with the tutor.*

Adre
Home, homeward > in the direction of home
Roedd yn braf mynd **adre** *ar ôl y gwyliau.*
It was nice to go **home** *after the holidays.*

Afal *[eg]*
> afalau
Apple
Dw i'n bwyta **afal** *i bwdin bob amser cinio.*
I eat an **apple** *for pudding every lunch-time.*

Afon *[eb]*
> afonydd
River
Afon *Hafren ac* **afon** *Dyfrdwy yw dwy* **afon** *fawr Cymru.*
The **river** *Severn and the* **river** *Dee are Wales' two big* **rivers**.

Agor
To open
Bydd y siop yn **agor** *fory am 08:00.*
The shop will **open** *tomorrow at 08:00.*

Agos
Close, near [Standard Welsh]
Mae Stadiwm y Mileniwm yn **agos** *i ganol Caerdydd.*
The Millennium Stadium is **near** *the centre of Cardiff.*
[See also > **Ar bwys** *and* **Wrth ymyl***]*

Angen *[eg]*
> anghenion
Need
Mae **angen** *help.*
There's a **need** *for help > help is needed.*

Anghofio
To forget
Pwy dych chi? Dw i wedi **anghofio** *eich enw chi!*
Who are you? I have **forgotten** *your name!*

Allan (i) *Out*
See > **Ma's**
(ii) *Exit*
Tân! Defnyddiwch y drws sy'n dweud **ALLAN**.
Fire! Use the door which says EXIT.

Am *About, at [+ time] + Treiglad Meddal*
Mae pawb yn hoffi siarad **am** *y tywydd yng Nghymru.*
Everyone likes to talk about the weather in Wales.
Bydd y ddrama'n dechrau **am dde**g *o'r gloch.*
The play will start at ten o'clock.

Ambiwlans *[eg]* *Ambulance*
> ambiwlansys *Ffonion nhw am* **ambiwlans** *ar ôl gweld y ddamwain.*
They phoned for an ambulance after seeing the accident.

Amgueddfa *[eb]* *Museum*
> amgueddfeydd *Mae llun y* Mona Lisa *yn* **amgueddfa'r** *Louvre,Paris.*
The picture of the Mona Lisa **is in the Louvre museum,** *Paris.*

Amser *[eg]* *Time*
> amserau *Dyn ni wedi mwynhau'n fawr, mae'r* **amser** *wedi hedfan.*
We've really enjoyed ourselves, the time has flown.

Anfon *To send* > *To send to =* anfon **at** *[people],* **i** *[place] [Standard Welsh]*
See > **Hala**

Anifail *[eg]*
> anifeiliaid

Animal
Does dim llawer o **anifeiliaid** *ar ei fferm e.*
There aren't many **animals** *on his farm.*

Anifail anwes

Pet
Mae llawer o bobl yn cadw ci fel **anifail anwes**.
Lots of people keep a dog as a pet.

Anifail gwyllt

Wild animal
Roedd y plentyn yn rhedeg o gwmpas fel **anifail gwyllt**.
The child was running about like a **wild animal**.

Annwyd *[eg]*

(a) Cold
Dw i ddim yn teimlo'n dda – mae **annwyd** *arna i.*
I don't feel well – I've got a **cold.**

Annwyl

(i) Cute
Mae'r gath fach yna'n **annwyl** *iawn.*
That little cat's very **cute.**
(ii) Dear
Annwyl *syr /* **Annwyl** *fadam...*
Dear *sir /* **Dear** *madam...*

Anodd

Difficult
Dydy'r treigladau yn Gymraeg ddim yn **anodd** *iawn.*
The mutations in Welsh aren't very **difficult.**

Anrheg *[eb]*
> anrhegion

Present, gift
Ar ei phen-blwydd cafodd hi lawer o **anrhegion** *hyfryd.*
On her birthday she had many wonderful **presents.**

Ar

On + Treiglad Meddal
Welaist ti'r rhaglen **ar** *y teledu neithiwr?*
Did you see the programme **on** *the television last night?*

14

*Mae'r bwyd yn barod – mae e **ar** y ford.*
The food's ready – it's on the table.
*Pawb ma's! Mae'r tŷ **ar** dân!*
Everybody out! The house is on fire!

Ar agor	*Open*
	*Mae'r siop **ar agor** trwy'r dydd.*
	The shop is open all day.
Ar ben	*Over, finished, at the end of*
	*Rwyt ti'n byw **ar ben** arall yr heol i fi.*
	You live at the other end of the road to me.
	*Does neb yma nawr – mae popeth **ar ben**.*
	There's nobody here now – everything's over / finished.
Ar bwys	*Close, near [Standard Welsh: **Agos**]*
	*Mae Stadiwm y Mileniwm **ar bwys** canol Caerdydd.*
	The Millennium Stadium is near the centre of Cardiff.
Ar eich traed!	*On your feet! Stand up!*
Ar gael	*Available*
	*Bydd coffi **ar gael** cyn y cyfarfod.*
	Coffee will be available before the meeting.
	*Pwy sy **ar gael** i weithio heno?*
	Who's available to work tonight?
Ar gau	*Closed*
	*Fel arfer, mae'r siop **ar gau** ar ddydd Sul.*
	Usually, the shop is closed on Sunday.
Ar hyn o bryd	*At the moment*
	Ar hyn o bryd does neb yma.
	At the moment there's nobody here.
Ar ôl	*(i) After*
	*Ble dych chi'n mynd **ar ôl** y gêm?*
	Where are you going after the game?
	(ii) Left, remaining
	*Mae pawb wedi bwyta'n dda – does dim bwyd **ar ôl**.*
	Everyone has eaten well – there's no food left.

Araf   *Slow*

*Mae'n rhaid i chi yrru'n **araf** yma.*

You must drive slowly here.

Arall   *Other*

> eraill   *Oes rhywun **arall** yn dod i'r dosbarth heno?*

**Is there anyone else (lit: anyone other)
coming to class tonight?**

*Oes, mae pobl **eraill** yn dod i'r dosbarth heno.*

**Yes, there are other people coming to class
tonight.**

Ardderchog   *Excellent*

*Yn ôl y tiwtor, mae gwaith y dysgwyr yn
ardderchog – maen nhw'n siarad yn dda
iawn.*

**According to the tutor, the learners' work is
excellent – they speak very well.**

Arholiad *[eg]*   *Exam*

> arholiadau   *Mae pawb yn mynd i wneud **arholiad** yn yr
haf.*

**Everyone's going to do an exam in the
summer.**

Arian *[eg]*   *Money*

*Dw i ddim yn gallu talu – does dim **arian**
gyda fi.*

I can't pay – I haven't got any money.

Arian cinio   *Dinner money*

*Mae'r athro'n gofyn am yr **arian cinio** bob bore Llun.*

**The teacher asks for dinner money every
Monday morning.**

Arian poced   *Pocket money*

*Dydy Siôn ddim yn cael llawer o **arian poced**, felly mae
e'n gweithio mewn caffi ar y penwythnos.*

**Siôn doesn't get much pocket money so he works in a
café at the weekend.**

Aros

(i) *To wait* > (*to wait* **for** = *aros* **am**)
Roedd llawer o bobl yn **aros** *am y bws i fynd i'r dre.*
Many people were **waiting** for the bus to go to town.
(ii) *To stay*
Dyn ni'n mynd i **aros** *mewn gwesty ar ein gwyliau.*
We are going to **stay** in a hotel on our holidays.

At

To [a person] + Treiglad Meddal
Ysgrifennais i lythyr **at** *fy modryb i ddiolch am yr anrheg.*
I wrote a letter **to** my auntie to say thank you for the present.
Anfonais y siec **at f**ab *fy chwaer.*
I sent the cheque **to** my sister's son.

Ateb *[eg]*
> atebion

An answer, a reply
Dw i ddim wedi cael **ateb** *i'r cwestiwn eto.*
I haven't had a **reply** to the question yet.

Ateb *[verb]*

To answer, to reply
Atebais *i dy lythyr y bore yma.*
I **answer**ed your letter this morning.

Athro *[eg]*
> athrawon

Teacher [male]

Athrawes *[eb]*
> athrawesau

Teacher [female]
Mae Mr Evans yn gweithio fel **athro** *Cymraeg.*
Mr Evans works as a Welsh **(male) teacher**.
Mae Mrs Jenkins yn gweithio fel **athrawes** *Saesneg.*
Mrs Jenkins works as an English **(female) teacher**.

Awr *[eb]*	**Hour**
> oriau	*Cyrhaeddon ni yma dros* **awr** *'nôl ond dyn ni ddim wedi gweld neb eto.*
	We arrived here over an hour ago but we haven't seen anyone yet.
Awst *[mis]*	*August*
	Fel arfer, dyn ni'n hoffi mynd i'r Eisteddfod ym mis **Awst**.
	Usually, we like to go to the Eisteddfod in August.

B

Baban *[eg]*	*Baby [See also >* **Babi***]*
> babanod	*neu*
Babi *[eg]*	*Ydy'r* **babi'n** *cysgu eto?*
> babis	**Is the baby sleeping yet?**
Bacwn *[eg]*	**Bacon**
	Bwyton ni wy, **bacwn** *a sglodion i ginio.*
	We ate egg, bacon and chips for lunch.
Bach	*Small, little*
	Enw fy mrawd **bach** *yw Ifan.*
	The name of my little brother is Ifan.
Bachgen *[eg]*	*Boy [Standard Welsh]*
> bechgyn	*See >* **Crwt[yn] / cryts**
Bag *[eg]*	*Bag*
> bagiau	*Pris* **bag** *siopa yng Nghymru yw pum ceiniog.*
	The price of a shopping bag in Wales is five pence.

Banc *[eg]*
> banciau

Bank
*Mae'n rhaid i fi alw yn y **banc** i gael arian.*
I have to call in the bank to get money.

Bant

Away, off [Standard Welsh: I ffwrdd]
*Aethon ni **bant** am wythnos o wyliau.*
We went away for a week's holiday.

Bant â chi!
Off with you / Off you go!

Bara *[eg]*

Bread
*Mae **bara** brown yn dda i chi.*
Brown bread is good for you.

Bara menyn

Bread and butter [also as an idiom]
*O na! Dim **bara menyn** i de eto!*
Oh no! Not bread and butter for tea again!
*Mae hi'n ennill ei **bara menyn** yn gweithio mewn siop.*
**She earns her bread and butter working in
a shop.**

Bara brith

*No English translation. (lit: speckled bread.
It's a kind of rich fruit loaf.)*

Bara lawr

Laver bread
*Mae marchnad Abertawe'n enwog am ei **bara lawr**.*
Swansea market is famous for its laver bread.

Bath *[eg]*

Bath
*Doedd y plant ddim yn hoffi amser **bath**.*
The children didn't like bath time.

Becso

To worry [Standard Welsh: Poeni]
*Peidiwch â **becso**! Bydd popeth yn iawn.*
Don't worry! Everything will be OK.

Beic *[eg]*
> beiciau

Bike
*Mae defnyddio **beic** yn dda i'r iechyd.*
Using a bike is good for your health.

Mynd ar gefn beic *To ride a bike*
*Aethon ni **ar gefn beic** i lawr i'r parc.*
*We **rode a bike** down to the park.*

Beiro *[eg/eb]* *Biro*
> beiros *Does dim llawer o **feiro** coch ar fy ngwaith cartre!*
*There's not much red **biro** on my homework!*

Bendigedig *Wonderful*
*Cawson ni barti **bendigedig** ar ei phen-blwydd yn 25 oed.*
*We had a **wonderful** party on her 25th birthday.*

Benthyg *To loan / Lend*
> rhoi benthyg i *Wnei di **roi benthyg** £50 i ni?*
*Will you **loan / lend** us £50?*

Cael benthyg *To borrow*
*Dych chi wedi **cael benthyg** £100 gyda fi'n barod!*
*You've already **borrowed** £100 from me!*

Benywaidd* *Feminine* > Enw benywaidd = *Feminine noun*
Beth? *What?*
Beth *yw enw tiwtor y cwrs?*
What *is the name of the course tutor?*

Bisgedi *Biscuits [ell]*
bisgïen *[eb]* *Dych chi'n hoffi **bisgedi** gyda'ch te?*
*Do you like **biscuits** with your tea?*

Ble? *Where?*
Ble *mae Siân a Dafydd yn byw?*
Where *do Siân and Dafydd live?*

Blino *To tire* > wedi blino = *tired*
Gweithion ni'n galed yn y dosbarth heno.
*Mae pawb **wedi blino**.*
*We worked hard in class tonight. Everyone is **tired**.*

Blwyddyn *[eb]*   *Year*
> blynyddoedd   *Dyn ni'n edrych ymlaen at ddod 'nôl y* **flwyddyn** *nesa.*
   We're looking forward to coming back next year.

Bod   *To be*
   Mae'n bwysig **bod** *yn y neuadd erbyn saith o'r gloch.*
   It's important to be in the hall by seven o'clock.

Bola *[eg]*   *Stomach, belly*
> boliau   *Dw i wedi bwyta gormod. Mae fy* **mola** *i'n llawn…*
   I've eaten too much. My stomach is full…

Bola tost   Stomach ache
   … ond does dim **bola tost** *gyda fi!*
   … but I haven't got **stomach ache!**

Bord *[eb]*   *Table*
> bordydd   *Dewch i eistedd wrth y* **ford** *– mae bwyd yn barod.*
   Come and sit at the table – food is ready.

Bore *[eg]*   *Morning*
> boreau   *Bydd hi'n bwrw glaw yn y* **bore** *ond bydd hi'n sych yn y prynhawn.*
   It will be raining in the morning but it will be dry in the afternoon.

Braf   *Fine [doesn't mutate]*
   Roedd y tywydd yn **braf** *pan aethon ni i Sbaen.*
   The weather was fine when we went to Spain.

Braich *[eb]*   *Arm*
> breichiau   *Torrodd Elin ei* **braich** *yn y ddamwain.*
   Elin broke her arm in the accident.

Brawd *[eg]*   *Brother*
> brodyr   *Mae un **brawd** gyda fi ac mae e'n byw yn Wrecsam.*

                 *I have one **brother** and he lives in Wrexham.*

Brawd yng nghyfraith *Brother-in-law*
                 *Enw fy **mrawd yng nghyfraith** (brawd fy ngwraig) yw Ifor.*

                 *My **brother-in-law** (my wife's brother)'s name is Ifor.*

Brawddeg* *[eb]*   *Sentence*
> brawddegau*

Brecwast *[eg]*   *Breakfast*
                 *Dw i'n hoffi bwyta **brecwast** yn y gwely bob dydd Sul.*

                 *I like to eat **breakfast** in bed every Sunday.*

Brechdan *[eb]*   *Sandwich*
> brechdanau   *Dyn ni'n mwynhau **brechdan** ham a chaws i ginio.*

                 *We enjoy a ham and cheese **sandwich** for lunch.*

Bron (yn)   *Almost*
                 *Mae'n hwyr iawn – mae hi **bron yn** un o'r gloch yn y bore.*

                 *It's very late – it's **almost** one o'clock in the morning.*

Brown   *Brown*
                 *Mae gwallt hir, **brown** gyda fy mam.*

                 *My mother has got long, **brown** hair.*

Brws[h] *[eg]*   *Brush*
> brwshys   *Maen nhw'n defnyddio eu **brwsh** dannedd bob tro.*

                 *They use their tooth**brush** every time.*

Brwsio   *To brush*
                 *Mae'r plant yn **brwsio** eu dannedd bob nos.*

                 *The children **brush** their teeth every night.*

Bwrdd *[eg]*   *Table [Standard Welsh]*
> byrddau   *See >* **Bord**
Bwrw glaw/eira   *To rain/snow*
                     Yn y bore, bydd hi'n **bwrw eira** *yn y mynyddoedd ond bydd hi'n* **bwrw glaw** *erbyn y prynhawn.*
                     In the morning, it will be **snowing** *in the mountains but by the afternoon it will be* **raining**.

Bws *[eg]*   *Bus*
> bysiau   *Mae'r* **bws** *yn mynd o ganol y dre i lawr i'r môr.*
                     The **bus** *goes from the town centre down to the sea.*

Bwyd *[eg]*   *Food*
> bwydydd   *Mae'n rhaid i ni fynd i'r siop – does dim* **bwyd** *ar ôl.*
                     We have to go to the shop – there's no **food** *left.*

Bwydo   *To feed*
                     Mae'r ffermwr yn **bwydo** *ei anifeiliaid.*
                     The farmer is **feeding** *his animals.*

Bwydlen *[eb]*   *Menu*
> bwydlenni   *Dw i ddim yn gwybod beth i fwyta – dw i'n mynd i edrych ar y* **fwydlen**.
                     I don't know what to eat – I'm going to look at the **menu**.

Bwyta   *To eat*
                     Fel arfer, dyn ni'n **bwyta** *am saith o'r gloch.*
                     Usually, we **eat** *at seven o'clock.*

Bwyta allan / ma's *To eat out*
                     Maen nhw'n **bwyta ma's** *unwaith yr wythnos.*
                     They **eat out** *once a week.*

Tŷ bwyta	*Restaurant*
	Maen nhw'n gwneud bwyd da yn y **tŷ bwyta** *newydd.*
	They do good food in the new restaurant.
Byr	*Short*
	Mae'n anodd rhoi ateb **byr** *i'r cwestiwn.*
	It's difficult to give a short answer to the question.
Bys *[eg]* > bysedd	*Finger* *Yn y ddamwain, collodd hi ei* **bys.**
	In the accident, she lost her finger.
Byth	*Ever / Never* *Dw i* **byth** *eisiau gweld y ffilm yna eto.*
	I never want to see that film again.
Cymru am **byth!**	*Wales for* **ever!**
Byw	*To live* *Dych chi wedi symud tŷ? Ble dych chi'n* **byw** *nawr?*
	Have you moved house? Where do you live now?

C

Cacen *[eb]* > cacennau	*Cake* *Prynon ni* **gacen** *siocled fawr ar ei pen-blwydd hi.*
	We bought a big chocolate cake on her birthday.
	[See also > **Teisen***]*
Cadair *[eb]* > cadeiriau	*Chair* *Roedd bord a phedair* **cadair** *yn y stafell fwyta.*

There was a table and four **chairs** in the dining room.

Cadw
To keep
Dyn nhw ddim yn **cadw** *eu car yn y garej.*
They don't **keep** their car in the garage.

Cadw'n heini
To keep fit
Mae dosbarth **cadw'n heini** *yn y ganolfan chwaraeon.*
There's a **keep fit** class in the sports centre.

Cael
To have, to get
Dw i'n **cael** *brecwast am saith o'r gloch fel arfer...*
Usually I **have** breakfast at seven o'clock...
... ond ddoe **ces i** *frecwast am wyth o'r gloch.*
... but yesterday I **had** breakfast at eight o'clock.

Caffi [eg]
Café
Maen nhw'n gwerthu coffi hyfryd yn y **caffi** *yma.*
They sell lovely coffee in this **café**.

Camera [eg]
> camerâu
Camera
Wyt ti'n gwybod sut mae'r **camera** *newydd yn gweithio?*
Do you know how the new **camera** works?

Canol [eg]
Centre, middle
Dydy **canol** *y dre ddim yn fawr iawn.*
The **centre** of the town / town **centre** isn't very big.

Yng nghanol
in the middle, centre of
Maen nhw'n adeiladu fflatiau newydd **yng nghanol** *y dre.*
They're building new flats **in the middle/centre** of town / in the town centre.

Canolfan [eb]   Centre (i.e. leisure, shopping, sports centre)
> canolfannau

Canolfan chwaraeon *Sports centre*
*Dyn ni'n chwarae hoci yn y **ganolfan chwaraeon**.*
We play hockey in the sports centre.

Canolfan hamdden *Leisure centre*
*Aeth y plant i'r **ganolfan hamdden** i nofio.*
The children went to the leisure centre to swim.

Canolfan siopa *Shopping centre*
*Roedd llawer o bobl yn y **ganolfan siopa** cyn y Nadolig.*
There were lots of people in the shopping centre
before *Christmas.*

Canu   *(i) To sing*
*Mae côr Aberheli'n **canu** yn Gymraeg.*
Aberheli choir sing in Welsh.
(ii) To ring [phone]
*Mae'r ffôn yn **canu**. Atebwch e!*
The phone's ringing. Answer it!

Capel [eg] *Chapel*
> capeli *Bydd y cyngerdd Nadolig yn y **capel** heno.*
The Christmas concert will be in the chapel tonight.

Car [eg] *Car*
> ceir *Dych chi'n gallu gadael y **car** yn y maes parcio.*
You can leave the car in the car park.

Carafán [eb] *Caravan*
> carafanau *Arhoson ni mewn **carafán** yr haf yma.*
We stayed in a caravan this summer.

Carden bost [eb] *Postcard [Standard Welsh: **Cerdyn post**]*
*Pob hwyl ar y gwyliau! Cofiwch anfon **carden bost**.*
All the best for the holidays! Remember to send a postcard!

Cardigan *[eb]*
> cardiganau

Cardigan
Yn y gaea, dw i'n gwisgo **cardigan** *bob dydd.*
In the winter, I wear a cardigan every day.

Cariad *[eg]*
> cariadon

(i) Boyfriend / Girlfriend / Lover
Mae **cariad** *Siân yn dod o'r Eidal.*
Siân's boyfriend comes from Italy.
Mae **cariad** *Ffred yn dod o'r Alban.*
Ffred's girlfriend comes from Scotland.
(ii) Love [noun]
Pen-blwydd hapus! Llawer o **gariad***, Mam a Dad.*
Happy birthday! Lots of love, Mum and Dad.

Cartre *[eg]*
> cartrefi

Home
Pob hwyl i chi yn eich **cartre** *newydd!*
All the best to you in your new home!
Enw'r **cartre** *hen bobl yw Bryn Awelon.*
The name of the old people's home is Bryn Awelon.

Gartre

At home
Ffoniwch fi **gartre** *ar ôl saith o'r gloch!*
Phone me at home after seven o'clock!

Caru

To love
Dw i'n dy **garu** *di.*
I love you.

Castell *[eg]*
> cestyll

Castle
Dych chi wedi gweld y **castell** *yng Nghaernarfon?*
Have you seen the castle in Caernarfon?

Cath *[eb]*
> cathod

Cat
Mae ein **cath** *ni'n hoffi yfed llaeth a chysgu.*
Our cat likes to drink milk and sleep.

Cau

To shut, close
Mae'r siop yn **cau** *am bump o'r gloch.*
The shop shuts at five o'clock.

Cawl *[eg]*   *Soup, broth, 'cawl'*
                           Mae'r plant yn hoffi bwyta **cawl** *a bara*
                           cartre.
                           **The children like eating cawl and home
                           made bread.**

Caws *[eg]*   *Cheese*
                           Caws *gwyn yw* **caws** *Caerffili.*
                           Caerphilly cheese is white cheese.

Cefn *[eg]*   *Back [of the body or of a place]*
> cefnau   *Eisteddon ni yn y* **cefn**.
                           We sat at the back.

Cefn tost   Backache
                           Dw i ddim yn gweithio – mae **cefn tost** *gyda fi.*
                           I'm not working – I've got backache.

Ceg *[eb]*   *Mouth*
> cegau   *Mae'r deintydd yn dweud: 'Agorwch eich* **ceg!'**
                           The dentist says: 'Open your mouth!'

Cegin *[eb]*   *Kitchen*
> ceginau   *Mae* **cegin** *fawr yn y tŷ newydd.*
                           There's a big kitchen in the new house.

Ceiniog *[eb]*   *Penny / pence*
> ceiniogau   *Pris y papur yw pum deg* **ceiniog**.
                           The price of the paper is fifty pence.

Cerdyn post *[eg]* Postcard *[Standard Welsh]*
> cardiau post   *See >* **Carden bost**

Cerdded   *To walk*
                           Mae'n rhaid i'r plant **gerdded** *i'r ysgol.*
                           The children must walk to school.

Ci *[eg]*   *Dog*
> cŵn   *Dw i'n mynd â'r* **ci** *am dro bob dydd.*
                           I take the dog for a walk every day.

Cig [eg]
> cigoedd

Meat
*Bwytais i'r **cig** ond dim y llysiau.*
I ate the meat but not the vegetables.

Cig eidion

Beef

Cig moch

Bacon [bacwn] or pork [porc]

Cig oen

Lamb

Cinio [eb/eg]
> ciniawau

Lunch / Dinner
*Byddwn ni'n bwyta **cinio** am un o'r gloch heddiw.*
We will be eating lunch at one o'clock today.

Cloc [eg]
> clociau

(i) Clock
*Mae'r **cloc** ar y wal yn araf.*
The clock on the wall is slow.
(ii) O'clock = O'r gloch
*Mae'n wyth **o'r gloch** – amser brecwast.*
It's eight o'clock – time for breakfast.

Clou [SW]

Quick / Quickly
*Rhedodd y ci yn **glou** iawn.*
The dog ran very quickly.

Clust [eb/eg]
> clustiau

Ear
*Gair yn eich **clust**, os gwelwch yn dda.*
A word in your ear, please.

Clust dost

Earache / A bad ear
*Dw i ddim yn clywed yn dda – mae **clust dost** gyda fi.*
I don't hear well – I've got earache / a bad ear.

Clwb [eg]
> clybiau

Club
*Mae **clwb** pêl-droed Abertawe'n chwarae yn y Liberty.*
Swansea football club play at the Liberty.

Clwb nos	*Night club*
	Bydd y **clwb nos** *ar agor tan ddau o'r gloch y bore.*
	The night club *will be open until two o'clock in the morning.*
Clywed	*To hear*
	Mae'n anodd **clywed** *y tiwtor yng nghefn y stafell.*
	It's difficult / hard to **hear** *the tutor at the back of the room.*
Coch	*Red*
	Yfais i ormod o win **coch** *neithiwr.*
	I drank too much **red** *wine last night.*
Codi	*(i) to get up*
	Faint o'r gloch dych chi'n **codi** *yn y bore?*
	What time do you **get up** *in the morning?*
	(ii) to pick / lift up / to raise
	Mae'n anodd **codi**'*r ci – mae e'n fawr.*
	It's difficult to **pick up** *the dog – he's big.*
	(iii) to go up
	Mae pris petrol wedi **codi**.
	The price of petrol has **gone up**.
Coes *[eb]*	*Leg*
> coesau	*Torrodd Eleri ei* **choes** *ar y mynydd.*
	Eleri broke her **leg** *on the mountain.*
Coes dost	A bad leg
Cofio	*To remember*
	Dw i ddim yn gallu **cofio** *ei enw e.*
	I can't remember his **name**.
Coffi *[eg]*	*Coffee*
	Dw i'n yfed **coffi** *mawr bob bore.*
	I drink a large **coffee** *every morning.*

Coginio	*To cook* [Standard Welsh]
	See > **Cwcan**
Coleg *[eg]*	*College*
> colegau	*Ar ôl gadael yr ysgol, mae hi eisiau mynd i'r* **coleg**.
	After leaving school, she wants to go to college.
Colli	*To lose*
	Collodd *Cymru 2–1 yn erbyn Ffrainc.*
	Wales lost 2–1 against France.
Côr *[eg]*	*Choir*
> corau	*Canodd y* **côr** *i godi arian i'r eisteddfod.*
	The choir sang to raise money for the eisteddfod.
Cot *[eb]*	*Coat*
> cotiau	*Bydd hi'n gwisgo* **cot** *trwy'r gaea.*
	She will be wearing a coat throughout the winter.
Cot law	*Raincoat*
	Mae hi'n bwrw glaw: dw i'n mynd i wisgo **cot law**.
	It's raining: I'm going to wear a **raincoat**.
Credu	*To believe, to think*
	Dw i ddim yn **credu** *eu stori nhw o gwbl.*
	I don't believe their story at all.
Croten *[eb]*	*Girl* [Standard Welsh: **Merch**]
> crotesi	*Fel* **croten** *fach, dw i'n cofio chwarae hoci yn yr ysgol.*
	As a small girl, I remember playing hockey at school.
Crwt / -yn *[eg]*	*Boy* [Standard Welsh: **Bachgen**]
> cryts	*Fel* **crwt** *bach, dw i'n cofio chwarae pêl-droed ar y stryd.*
	As a small boy, I remember playing football in the street.

Cwcan To cook *[Standard Welsh: Coginio]*
Mae fy ffrind i'n **cwcan** *pasta bob nos.*
***My friend* cooks** *pasta every night.*

Cwestiwn *[eg]* *Question*
> cwestiynau *Doedd y tiwtor ddim yn gallu ateb y*
cwestiwn.
The tutor couldn't answer the **question**.

Cwpla To finish *[Standard Welsh: Gorffen]*
(i) Dych chi wedi **cwpla** *bwyta eto?*
***Have you* finished** *eating yet?*
(ii) Bydd y cwrs yn **cwpla** *mewn tair*
wythnos.
The course will be **finishing** *in three weeks.*
[Alternative in SW > Bennu]

Cwrdd [â] *[verb]* To meet *[Standard Welsh: Cyfarfod]*
Dyn ni'n **cwrdd** â *Siân yn y maes parcio.*
We're **meeting** *Siân in the car park.*

Cwrs *[eg]* *Course*
> cyrsiau *Roedd y* **cwrs** *yn dda iawn. Dysgon ni lawer*
o eiriau newydd.
The **course** *was very good. We learnt lots of*
new words.

Cwrw *[eg]* *Beer*
Mae'r dafarn yn gwerthu **cwrw** *o Gymru.*
The pub sells **beer** *from Wales.*

Cychwyn *To start*
Mae'r daith yn **cychwyn** *yn Wrecsam.*
The trip **starts** *in Wrexham.*

Cyfan* *All, everything*

Cyfarfod *[eg]* *A meeting*
> cyfarfodydd *Bydd y* **cyfarfod** *yn neuadd y dre.*
The **meeting** *will be in the town hall.*

Cyfarfod *[verb]* *To meet*
See > Cwrdd â

32

Cyfeiriad *[eg]*   *Address*
> cyfeiriadau   *Dyn ni wedi symud tŷ. Dych chi eisiau'r*
                    cyfeiriad *newydd?*
                    We have moved house. Do you want the new
                    address*?*

Cyfieithu*   *To translate* > **Cyfieithwch!** *= Translate!*
Cyflym   *Quick / Quickly*
                    See > **Clou**

Cyfrifiadur *[eg]* *Computer*
> cyfrifiaduron   *Dydy'r* **cyfrifiadur** *ddim yn gweithio! Dyn*
                    ni wedi colli popeth!
                    The **computer** *isn't working. We've lost*
                    everything!

Cyngerdd *[eg/eb]* *Concert*
> cyngherddau   *Canodd Katherine Jenkins yn y* **gyngerdd**
                    fawr yng Nghaerdydd.
                    Katherine Jenkins sang in the big **concert** *in*
                    Cardiff.

Cymraeg   *(i) Welsh language [adjective]*
                    Rhaglen **Gymraeg** *yw Pobol y Cwm.*
                    Pobol y Cwm is a **Welsh (language)**
                    programme.
                    (ii) Welsh language [noun]
                    Oes rhywun yn siarad **Cymraeg** *yn y swyddfa?*
                    Does anyone speak **Welsh** *in the office?*

Cymro *[eg]*   *Welsh / A Welshman*
Cymraes *[eb]* *Welsh / A Welsh woman*
> Cymry   *The Welsh*
                    Cymro *yw Ifan – mae e'n dod o Fangor yn*
                    wreiddiol.
                    Ifan is **Welsh** *(i.e. a Welshman) – he comes*
                    from Bangor originally.

Cymraes *yw Eleri – mae hi'n dod o Bontypridd yn wreiddiol.*

*Eleri is **Welsh** (i.e. a Welsh woman) – she comes from Pontypridd originally.*

Cymru *[eb]*   *Wales*

*Bydd y rhaglen ar BBC **Cymru** heno.*

*The programme will be on BBC **Wales** tonight.*

Cymryd   *To take (i.e. to receive, accept)*

*Dych chi'n **cymryd** siwgr a llaeth yn eich coffi?*

*Do you **take** sugar and milk in your coffee?*

Cymylog   *Cloudy*

*Mae'n **gymylog** iawn heddiw ond dydy hi ddim yn bwrw glaw eto.*

*It's very **cloudy** today but it isn't raining yet.*

Cyn   *Before*

*Bydd pawb yn cyrraedd **cyn** deg o'r gloch.*

*Everyone will arrive **before** ten o'clock.*

Cyn bo hir   Soon, before long

Maen nhw wedi gadael y tŷ ond byddan nhw 'nôl **cyn bo hir**.

They've left the house but they will be back **soon**.

Cynnar   *Early*

*Gadawodd y trên yn hwyr ond cyrhaeddon ni'n **gynnar**.*

*The train left late but we arrived **early**.*

Cyrraedd   *To arrive [at / in]*

*Byddwn ni'n **cyrraedd** Sbaen yn y prynhawn.*

*We'll be **arriving** in Spain in the afternoon.*

Cyrri *[eg]*   *Curry*

> cyrïau   *Mae'r **cyrri**, Vindaloo, yn dwym iawn.*

*The **curry**, Vindaloo, is very hot.*

Cysgu   *To sleep*
*Aeth y babi i **gysgu**'n syth ar ôl bwyd.*
The baby went to sleep straight away after food.

Cyw iâr *[eg]*   *Chicken*
> cywion ieir   *See > **Ffowlyn***

CH

Chi   *You [formal singular]*
(i) You
*Bore da, Mrs Jones. Sut dych **chi** heddiw?*
Good morning, Mrs Jones. How are you today?
(ii) You [formal and informal plurals]
*Siwan a Lowri, dych **chi**'n barod?*
Siwan and Lowri, are you ready?
*(iii) Your [formal singular and plural] (+ **eich**)*
*Ydy eich plant **chi**'n mynd i ysgol Gymraeg?*
Do your children go to a Welsh (language) school?

Chwaer *[eb]*   *Sister*
> chwiorydd   *Mae dwy **chwaer** gyda fi ac maen nhw'n byw yn y Rhondda.*
I have two sisters and they live in the Rhondda.

Chwaer yng nghyfraith   *Sister-in-law*
*Enw fy **chwaer yng nghyfraith** (chwaer fy ngwraig) yw Mair.*
My sister-in-law (my wife's sister)'s name is Mair.

Chwarae	*To play*
	Roedd y plant yn mwynhau **chwarae** *gyda eu teganau.*
	The children were enjoying playing with their toys.
Chwaraeon [ell]	*Sports, games*
	Maen nhw'n dysgu llawer o **chwaraeon** *yn yr ysgol.*
	They learn lots of sports in school.
Chwarter [eg]	*Quarter*
	Bydd pawb yma mewn **chwarter** *awr.*
	Everyone will be here in a quarter of an hour.
Chwefror [mis]	*February*
	Mis rhif dau yw mis **Chwefror.**
	***February** is month number two.*
Chwith	*Left*
	Trowch i'r **chwith** *ar ôl yr ysgol...*
	Turn to the left after the school...
	... ac mae ein tŷ ni ar y **chwith.**
	*... **and our house is on the left.***

D

Da	*Good / Well*
	Mae côr Aberheli yn gôr **da...**
	Côr Aberheli is a good choir...
	... maen nhw'n canu'n **dda.**
	*... **they sing well.***
Damwain [eb]	*Accident*
> damweiniau	*Digwyddodd y* **ddamwain** *am ddeg o'r gloch neithiwr.*
	***The accident** happened at ten o'clock last night.*
Dan	*Under + Treiglad Meddal*

Roedd y ci'n chwarae **dan** *y ford.*
The dog was playing under the table.
Aeth y ci **dan g**ar fy mrawd.
The dog went under my brother's car.

Dangos
To show > *to show someone something =*
dangos rhywbeth **i** *rywun*
Bydd S4C yn **dangos** *y ffilm am Richard*
Burton fory.
**S4C will show the film about Richard Burton
tomorrow.**

Dant *[eg]*
> dannedd
Tooth
Dyn ni'n glanhau ein **dannedd** *bob nos.*
We clean our teeth every night.

Darllen
To read
Dw i'n **darllen** *y papur bob dydd.*
I read the paper every day.

Darllen am
To read **about**
Darllenais i **am** *y ddamwain yn y papur.*
I read about *the accident in the paper.*

Dawns *[eb]*
> dawnsfeydd
Dance
Bydd **dawns** *fawr yn neuadd y pentre heno.*
**There will be a big dance in the village hall
tonight.**

Dawnsio
To dance
Rwyt ti'n mynd i **ddawnsio** *yn y sioe.*
You're going to dance in the show.

De *[eg]*
South
Mae Mam yn dod o'r **de** *yn wreiddiol.*
My mother comes from the south originally.

De *[eb]*
Right (i.e. opposite to 'left')
Trowch i'r **dde** *ar ôl y capel...*
Turn to the right after the chapel...

*... ac mae ein tŷ ni ar y **dde**.*

*... and out house is on the **right**.*

Deall — *To understand*

*Dw i ddim yn eich **deall** chi. Dych chi'n siarad yn rhy gyflym.*

*I don't **understand** you. You're speaking too fast.*

Dechrau — *To begin*

*Pryd mae'r gyngerdd yn **dechrau**?*

*When does the concert **begin**?*

Defnyddio — *To use*

*Dyn ni ddim yn gallu **defnyddio**'r peiriant golchi newydd.*

*We can't **use** the new washing machine.*

Deffro — *To wake up [South Wales: **Dihuno**]*

*Dydy Alun ddim wedi **deffro** eto: mae e'n cysgu yn y gwely.*

*Alun hasn't **woken up** yet: he's sleeping in bed.*

Deialog *[eb]** — *Dialogue*

Deintydd *[eg]* — *Dentist*

> deintyddion — *Bydd y **deintydd** yn edrych ar fy nannedd y prynhawn yma.*

*The **dentist** will be looking at my teeth this afternoon.*

Diddordeb *[eg]* — *Interest*

> diddordebau — *Beth yw eich **diddordebau** chi?*

*What are your **interests**?*

Diflas — *Miserable [can also mean 'boring' e.g. see > **Drama**]*

*Roedd hi'n **ddiflas** ddoe, yn bwrw glaw trwy'r dydd.*

*It was **miserable** yesterday, raining all day.*

Digon (o)   *Enough (of)*
*Dych chi wedi cael **digon** o fwyd? Dych chi wedi cael **digon**?*
Have you had enough food? Have you had enough?

Digwydd   *To happen*
*Beth sy'n **digwydd** yn y dre heno?*
What's happening in town tonight?

Dihuno   *To wake up*
*Dydy Alun ddim wedi **dihuno** eto: mae e'n cysgu yn y gwely.*
Alun hasn't woken up yet: he's sleeping in bed.

Dillad *[ell]*   *Clothes*
*Roedd Mam-gu'n golchi'r **dillad** bob dydd Llun.*
My gran used to wash the clothes every Monday.

Dillad chwaraeon   *Sportswear/clothes*
*Byddwn ni'n gwisgo **dillad chwaraeon** yn y dosbarth cadw'n heini heno.*
We will be wearing sportswear in the keep fit class tonight.

Dillad nofio   *Swimwear*
*Gwisgodd hi ei **dillad nofio** yn y pwll nofio.*
She wore her swimwear in the swimming pool.

Dillad nos   *Nightwear*
*Dyn ni'n gwisgo **dillad nos** yn y gwely.*
We wear nightwear in bed.

Dim / Ddim   *Used to make the negative.*
*Does **dim** arian gyda fi.*
I have not / I haven't got any money.

Dim

No / Not [+ a noun]
Dim *Saesneg yn y dosbarth –* **dim** *un gair o Saesneg!*
No *English in class –* **not** *one word of English!*
Popeth yn iawn, **dim** *problem o gwbl.*
Everything's fine, **no** *problem at all.*

Dim ond

Only
Faint o bobl oedd yn y dosbarth? **Dim ond** *Rhys a fi.*
How many people were in class? **Only** *Rhys and me.*

Dim (byd)

Nothing / Anything
Ddwedais i **ddim byd.**
I said **nothing** */ I didn't say* **anything.**

Diod *[eb]*
> diodydd

Drink [noun]
Bydd bwyd a **diod** *yn y parti.*
There will be food and **drink** *in the party.*
Dw i'n hoffi cael **diod** *gyda fy mwyd.*
I like to have a **drink** *with my food.*

Diolch *[i]*

Thank you
Dw i'n hoffi'r anrheg. **Diolch** *yn fawr* **i** *chi!*
I like the present. **Thank you** *very much /*
Many **thanks to you***!*

Dis *[eg]*

Dice
Pwy sy'n mynd nesa? Mae'r **dis** *gyda fi.*
Who goes next? I've got the **dice***!*

Dish[g]led *[eg/eb] A cup of / A cuppa [Standard Welsh:*
Paned*] Dyn ni'n cael* **dishgled** *bob dydd yn y dosbarth.*
We have a **cuppa** *every day in class.*
Dych chi eisiau **dishgled** *o de?*
Do you want a **cup of** *tea?*

Di-waith
Unemployed, out of work
*Dydy e ddim yn gweithio nawr. Mae e'n **ddi-waith**.*
He's not working now. He's unemployed / out of work.

Diwedd *[eg]*
End, finish
*Roedd **diwedd** y ffilm yn drist.*
The end of the film was sad.

Diwetha
Last (i.e. most recent)
*Daeth y llythyr ddydd Llun **diwetha**.*
The letter came last Monday.

Diwrnod *[eg]*
Day
*Dw i ddim yn cofio'r **diwrnod** cynta yn yr ysgol.*
I don't remember the first day at school.
*Dim gwaith fory! Mae **diwrnod** bant gyda fi.*
No work tomorrow! I've got a day off.

Dod
To come
*O ble dych chi'n **dod** yn wreiddiol?*
Where do you come from originally?

Dod â
To bring
*Maen nhw'n **dod** â'r anrheg gyda nhw.*
They're bringing the present with them.

Dodi
*To put [Standard Welsh: (ii) **Rhoi**]*
*Maen nhw'n **dodi**'r arian ar y ford.*
They put the money on the table.

Doli *[eb]*
> doliau
Dolly
*Roedd Megan eisiau cael **doli** newydd y Nadolig yma.*
Megan wanted to have a new dolly this Christmas.

Dosbarth *[eg]*
> dosbarthiadau
Class
*Dyn ni'n dysgu Cymraeg yn y **dosbarth**.*
We learn Welsh in class.

Dosbarth babanod   *Infants class*
Mae Ifan yn 7 ac mae e yn y **dosbarth babanod**.
Ifan is 7 and he is in the infants' class.

Dosbarth derbyn   *Reception class*
Mae Elin yn 5 ac mae hi yn y **dosbarth derbyn**.
Elin is 5 and she is in the reception class.

Dosbarth nos   *Night class*
Dyn ni'n dysgu Cymraeg mewn **dosbarth nos**.
We are learning Welsh in a night class.

Drama *[eb]*   *Play, drama*
> dramâu   *Es i i gysgu yn y* **ddrama** *– roedd hi'n ddiflas iawn.*
I went to sleep in the **play** *– it was very boring.*

Dringo   *To climb*
Byddwn ni'n **dringo**'r *mynydd fory.*
We will be **climbing** *the mountain tomorrow.*

Dros   *Over + Treiglad Meddal*
Maen nhw'n byw **dros** *y bont.*
They live **over** *the bridge.*
Es i **dros B**ont Hafren.
I went **over** *the Severn Bridge.*

Drwg   *(i) Bad / Naughty*
Mae plant Aberheli yn **ddrwg** *iawn.*
The Aberheli children are very **naughty / bad.**
(ii) Sorry
Mae'n ddrwg iawn gyda fi *ond dw i ddim yn deall.*
I'm very sorry *but I don't understand.*

Drws *[eg]*   *Door*
> drysau   *Aethon ni trwy'r* **drws** *i mewn i'r tŷ.*
We went through the **door** *into the house.*

Drws ffrynt / cefn *Front / Back door*
Dych chi'n mynd i mewn trwy'r **drws ffrynt** *a ma's trwy'r* **drws cefn**.
You go in through the **front door** *and out through the* **back door.**

Du *Black*
Dw i'n hoffi yfed coffi **du**, *heb laeth.*
I like drinking **black** *coffee, without milk.*

Dweud *To say*
Sut dych chi'n **dweud** *X yn Gymraeg?*
How do you **say** *X in Welsh?*

Dweud wrth *To tell*
Dwyt ti ddim wedi **dweud** *popeth* **wrth** *yr heddlu.*
You haven't **told** *the police everything.*

Dŵr *[eg]* *Water*
Roedd **dŵr** *yr afon yn oer iawn.*
The **water** *from the river was very cold.*

Dwylo *See >* **Llaw**
Dwyrain *[eg]* *East*
Mae'r haul yn codi yn y **dwyrain**.
The sun rises in the **east.**

Dy *[+ di]* *Your [informal singular] + Treiglad Meddal*
Ddest ti i'r dosbarth yn **dy** *gar di?*
Did you come to class in **your** *car?*

Dydd *[eg]* *Day [See also > individual days of the week]*
> dyddiau *Dyn ni'n mynd i'r dosbarth bob* **dydd**.
We go to class every **day.**

Dyfalu* *To guess*
Dyma *(i) Here is / are + Treiglad Meddal*
Dyma *lyfr da am arddio.*
Here's *a good book about gardening.*
(ii) This is [introducing someone] + Treiglad Meddal

Dyma *fy mam.*
This is *my mother.*

Dyn *[eg]*
> dynion

Man
Pwy yw'r **dyn** *newydd yn y dosbarth?*
Who is the new **man** *in class?*

Dyna

(i) There is / are + Treiglad Meddal
Dyna *ni.*
There *we* **are**.
(ii) How + adjective + Treiglad Meddal
Dyna **dd**iflas!
There's *miserable!* = **How** *miserable!*
(iii) That is + Treiglad Meddal
Dyna **f**am y plentyn.
That's *the child's mother.*

Dysgu

To learn [Also: to teach]
Dyn ni'n **dysgu** *Cymraeg yn y dosbarth.*
We **learn** *Welsh in class.*
Mae'r tiwtor yn **dysgu** *Cymraeg i ni.*
The tutor is **teaching** *us Welsh.*

Dysgwr *[eg]*
Dysgwraig *[eb]*
> dysgwyr

Learner
[Female] Learner
Siaradwch yn araf, os gwelwch yn dda,
dysgwr *dw i.*
Speak slowly, please, I am a **learner**.
Dysgwraig *o Gasnewydd yw Elin.*
Elin is a **female learner** *from Newport.*

DD

Ddoe

Yesterday
Es i i siopa yn y dre **ddoe**.
I went shopping in town **yesterday**.

E

E-bost
E-mail
Ces i e-bost am y cwrs newydd.
I received an e-mail about the new course.

E-bostio
To e-mail
Dw i'n e-bostio fy nhiwtor am y gwaith cartre.
I am e-mailing my tutor about the homework.

Ebrill *[mis]*
April
Mis rhif pedwar yw mis Ebrill.
April *is month number four.*

Echdoe
The day before yesterday
Roedd hi'n oer iawn echdoe.
It was very cold the day before (yesterday).

Edrych (ar)
To look [at] / Watch
Mae'r ci'n edrych yn hapus.
The dog looks happy.
Byddwn ni'n edrych ar y teledu heno.
We will be watching / looking at the television tonight.

Efallai
Perhaps [Standard Welsh]
See > Falle

Eglwys *[eb]*
> eglwysi
Church
Maen nhw'n mynd i'r eglwys bob dydd Sul.
They go to church every Sunday.

Ei *[benywaidd]*
Her + Treiglad Llaes / H- before vowels
Mae Laura'n cael ei pharti pen-blwydd heddiw.
Laura's having her birthday party today.
Mae hi'n hoffi ei hanrhegion hi.
She likes her presents.

Ei *[gwrywaidd]* *His + Treiglad Meddal*
*Mae e'n cael **ei b**arti pen-blwydd heddiw.*
*He's having **his** birthday party today.*

Eich *Your [formal singular / plural and informal plural]*
*Ydy **eich** plant chi'n mynd i ysgol Gymraeg?*
*Do **your** children go to a Welsh (language) school?*

Ein *Our + H- before vowels*
*Mae **ein** tŷ ni yng nghanol y dre.*
Our *house is in the middle of town.*
*Diolch yn fawr am **ein h**anrheg ni.*
*Thanks very much for **our** present.*

Eira *[eg]* *Snow*
*(i) Mae popeth yn wyn gyda'r **eira** i gyd.*
*Everything is white with all the **snow**.*
*(ii) Roedd hi'n **bwrw eira** yn yr Alban neithiwr.*
*It was **snowing** in Scotland last night.*

Eisiau *To want [Standard Welsh]*
See > **Moyn**

Eistedd *To sit*
*Ro'n i'n **eistedd** yn y dosbarth am ddwy awr.*
*I was **sitting** in class for two hours.*

Eisteddfod *[eb]* *Eisteddfod*
> eisteddfodau *Bydd yr **eisteddfod** yn mynd i'r gogledd eleni.*
*The **eisteddfod** will be going to the north this year.*

Eitha *Quite*
*Mae hi'n **eitha** oer yn y neuadd.*
*It's **quite** cold in the hall.*

Eleni *This year*
*Ble dych chi'n mynd ar eich gwyliau **eleni**?*
*Where are you going on your holidays **this year**?*

Ennill	*To win*
	*Pwy fydd yn **ennill** y rygbi eleni?*
	Who will win the rugby this year?
	*Y llynedd, **enillodd** Cymru.*
	Last year, Wales won.
Enw *[eg]*	*Name*
> enwau	*Beth yw eich **enw** chi?*
	What's your name?
Enwog	*Famous*
	*Mae Anthony Hopkins yn actor **enwog**.*
	Anthony Hopkins is a famous actor.
Erbyn	*By [especially with time]*
	*Dewch i'r parti **erbyn** wyth o'r gloch.*
	Come to the party by eight o'clock.
Erbyn hyn	*By now*
	Erbyn hyn, *mae pawb wedi mynd.*
	Everybody's gone by now.
(Yn) erbyn	*Against*
	*Y gêm fawr yw Cymru **yn erbyn** Lloegr.*
	The big game is Wales against England.
Erioed	*Ever / Never*
	*Dw i **erioed** wedi gweld Pobol y Cwm.*
	I've never seen Pobol y Cwm.
	*Dych chi wedi gweld Pobol y Cwm **erioed**?*
	Have you ever seen Pobol y Cwm?
Ers	*Since*
	*Dw i'n aros yma **ers** naw o'r gloch.*
	I am waiting (= I've been waiting) here since nine o'clock.
Ers pryd / faint	*Since when / How long*
	Ers pryd / ers faint *dych chi'n aros yma?*
	(Since when) How long have you been waiting here?

Esgusodwch fi!	*Excuse me!*
	Esgusodwch fi! *Ble mae'r dosbarth Cymraeg?*
	Excuse me! *Where is the Welsh class?*
Eto	*(i) Yet*
	*Dydy hi ddim wedi gwneud y gwaith **eto**.*
	*She hasn't done the work **yet**.*
	*(ii) Again [See > **Unwaith**]*
Eu	*Their + H- before vowels*
	*Mae **eu** car nhw yn y maes parcio.*
	***Their** car is in the car park.*
	*Faint yw **eu h**oed nhw?*
	*What is **their** age? / How old are they?*
Ewythr *[eg]*	*Uncle [Also: **Wncwl**]*
> ewythredd	*Doedd fy **ewythr** ddim yn medru siarad Cymraeg.*
	*My **uncle** couldn't speak Welsh.*

F

Faint?	*How much? How many? [Standard Welsh]*
	Faint *o blant sy yn y dosbarth?*
	How many *children are in the class?*
	Faint *o'r gloch yw hi?*
	*What time is it? (lit: **How much** o'clock is it?)*
	*[See also > **Sawl**]*
Falle	*Perhaps [Standard Welsh: **Efallai**]*
	Falle *bydd e'n cyrraedd heddiw.*
	Perhaps *he'll be arriving today.*
Fe / e	*(i) He*
	*Roedd **e**'n chwarae pêl-droed.*
	***He** was playing football.*

	(ii) His [+ ei]
	Beth yw ei gyfeiriad e?
	What is his address?
Fel	*(i) Like*
	Mae'r mab yn edrych fel ei dad.
	The son looks like his father.
	(ii) As
	Mae hi'n gweithio fel athrawes.
	She works as a teacher.
Fel arfer	*Usually*
	Mae'r dosbarth yn gorffen am naw fel arfer.
	The class usually finishes at nine.
Fi / i	*(i) Me, I*
	Fi yw'r person cynta i gyrraedd.
	I'm / it's me who is the first person to arrive.
	Mae'n rhaid i fi roi'r arian i Siôn.
	I must give the money to Siôn e.e. there's a need to me to give the money to Siôn.
	Esgusodwch fi!
	Excuse me!
	(ii) My [+ fy]
	Mae fy nhad i wedi prynu tŷ newydd.
	My father has bought a new house.
Fideo [eg]	*Video*
> fideos	*Maen nhw'n gwneud fideo o gyngerdd yr ysgol.*
	They are making a video of the school concert.
Fy	*My + Treiglad Trwynol*
	Mae fy nghar i wedi torri i lawr.
	My car has broken down.

FF

Ffatri *[eb]*
> ffatrïoedd

Factory
*Bydd y **ffatri**'n cau yn yr haf.*
The factory *will be closing in the summer.*

Ffeil *[eb]*
> ffeiliau

File
*Dw i wedi colli fy **ffeil** gwaith cartre.*
*I've lost my homework **file**.*

Ffenest[r] *[eb]*
> ffenestri

Window
*Agorwch y **ffenest** - mae'n dwym yma!*
*Open the **window** – it's hot here!*

Fferm *[eb]*
> ffermydd

Farm
Maen nhw'n cadw llawer o anifeiliaid ar y
fferm.
*They keep many animals on the **farm**.*

Ffermio

To farm
*Mae llawer o bobl yng Nghymru yn **ffermio**.*
*Many people in Wales **farm**.*

Ffermwr *[eg]*
> ffermwyr

Farmer
*Does dim llawer o arian gyda'r **ffermwr**.*
*The **farmer** hasn't got a lot of money.*

Ffilm *[eb]*
> ffilmiau

Film
Ffilm *Gymraeg yw Hedd Wyn.*
*Hedd Wyn is a Welsh (language) **film**.*

Fflat *[eb]*
> fflatiau

Flat
*Ro'n nhw'n byw mewn **fflat** yng nghanol y*
dre.
*They were living in a **flat** in the middle of*
town.

Bloc o fflatiau

A block of flats
*Ro'n nhw'n byw mewn **bloc o fflatiau** yng nghanol y dre.*
*They were living in a **block of flats** in the middle of town.*

Ffliw *[eg]*

Flu

*Roedd hi'n dost iawn – roedd **y ffliw** arni hi.*

She was very ill – she had flu.

Ffôn *[eg]*
> ffonau

Phone [noun]

Ffôn symudol

Mobile phone

*Collodd hi ei **ffôn symudol** newydd.*

She lost her new mobile phone.

Rhif ffôn

Phone number

*Beth yw eich **rhif ffôn** chi?*

What's your phone number?

Ffonio

To phone

*Mae Aled yn mynd i **ffonio** pawb yn y dosbarth.*

Aled's going to phone everyone in the class.

Ffordd *[eb]*
> ffyrdd

(i) Way

*Maen nhw ar y **ffordd** i'r dosbarth.*

They are on the way to class.

(ii) Road

*See > **Heol** [Standard Welsh]*

Ffowlyn *[eg]*
> ffowls

*Chicken [Standard Welsh: **Cyw iâr**]*

*Maen nhw'n cael **ffowlyn** a sglodion i swper.*

They're having chicken and chips for supper.

Ffrainc

France

*Dyn ni'n hoff iawn o win o **Ffrainc**.*

We're very fond of wine from France.

Ffrind *[eg]*
> ffrindiau

Friend

*Mae Ieuan yn **ffrind** da i fi...*

Ieuan is a good friend to me...

Ffrind gorau

Best friend

*... ond Iestyn yw fy **ffrind gorau**.*

... but Iestyn is my best friend.

G

Gadael	*To leave, depart*
	Am faint o'r gloch mae'r trên yn **gadael** *yr orsaf?*
	What time does the train leave / depart *from the station?*
Gaea *[eg]*	*Winter*
	Weithiau, mae'n bwrw eira yn y **gaea.**
	Sometimes, it snows in **winter.**
Gair *[eg]*	*Word*
> geiriau	*Deallais i bob* **gair** *yn y rhaglen.*
	I understood every **word** *in the programme.*
Galw	*To call*
	Bydd Dafydd yn **galw** *ar ôl ei ddosbarth.*
	Dafydd will be **calling** *after his class.*
Gallu	*To be able to / Can*
	Dw i ddim yn **gallu** *gweld y car.*
	I **can't** *see the car / I am not* **able to** *see the car.*
Gan	*Used to form the 'have / got' construction = 'with' in Standard Welsh*
	Mae **gan** *Catrin ddau o blant.*
	Catrin **has got** *two children (lit: There are two children* **with** *Catrin).*
	[See also > **Gyda***]*
Gardd *[eb]*	*Garden*
> gerddi	*Maen nhw'n hapus yn eistedd yn yr* **ardd.**
	They're happy sitting in the **garden.**
Garddio	*To garden, to do the gardening*
	Doedd hi ddim yn hoffi **garddio...**
	She didn't like **gardening...**

Garddwr *[eg]*   *Gardener*
> garddwyr   *... felly ffoniodd hi'r **garddwr**.*
    ... so she phoned the gardener.

Garej *[eg]*   *Garage*
> garejys   *Mae'r car yn y **garej** heno.*
    The car is in the garage tonight.
    *Dyn ni'n mynd i'r **garej** i brynu petrol.*
    We're going to the garage to buy petrol.

Geirfa *[eb]**   *Vocabulary*

Gêm *[eb]*   *Game*
> gemau   *Bydd y **gêm** rhwng Abertawe a Chaerdydd*
    yn bwysig iawn.
    The game between Swansea and Cardiff will
    be very important.
    *Mae'r plant yn hoffi chwarae **gemau***
    cyfrifiadur.
    The children like playing computer games.

Glanhau   *To clean*
    *Bydda i'n **glanhau**'r tŷ ddydd Sadwrn.*
    I will be cleaning the house on Saturday.

Glas   *Blue*
    *Mae Siân yn gwisgo cardigan **las** heddiw.*
    Siân is wearing a blue cardigan today.

Glaw *[eg]*   *Rain*
    *(i) Mae popeth yn wlyb iawn ar ôl y **glaw**.*
    Everything is very wet after the rain.
    *(ii) Roedd hi'n **bwrw glaw** yn y gogledd*
    neithiwr.
    It was raining in the north last night.

Gofyn (i)   *To ask*
    *Dw i eisiau **gofyn** cwestiwn am y daflen waith.*
    I want to ask a question about the worksheet.
    *Dw i'n mynd i **ofyn** i'r tiwtor.*
    I'm going to ask the tutor.

Gogledd *[eg]*   *North*
*Mae pobl y **gogledd** yn dweud 'efo' am 'gyda'.*
*The people from the **north** say 'efo' for 'gyda'.*

Golchi   *To wash (something) [See > **Ymolchi** for 'wash yourself']*
*Wyt ti'n **golchi** dy wallt heno?*
*Are you **washing** your hair tonight?*

Golff *[eg]*   *Golf*
*Dw i'n mwynhau chwarae **golff** bob dydd Sadwrn.*
*I enjoy playing **golf** every Saturday.*

Gorffen   *To finish [Standard Welsh]*
*See > **Cwpla***

Gorffennaf *[mis]*   *July*
*Mis rhif saith yw mis **Gorffennaf**.*
***July** is month number seven.*

Gorllewin *[eg]*   *West*
*Mae'r haul yn mynd i lawr yn y **gorllewin**.*
*The sun goes down in the **west**.*

Gormod (o)   *Too much*
*Dydy hi ddim eisiau pwdin. Mae hi wedi bwyta **gormod**.*
*She doesn't want pudding. She has eaten **too much**.*
*Maen nhw wedi yfed **gormod** o win.*
*They've drunk **too much** wine.*

Gorsaf *[eb]*   *Station*
> gorsafoedd

Gorsaf betrol   *Petrol station*
*Mae'r **orsaf betrol** yn gwerthu popeth.*
*The **petrol station** sells everything.*

Gorsaf fysiau   *Bus station*
*Bydda i'n teithio o **orsaf fysiau** Port Talbot.*
*I will be travelling from Port Talbot **bus station**.*

Gorsaf dân
Fire station
Bydd **gorsaf dân** *newydd Pontypandy yng nghanol y dre.*
Pontypandy's new fire station *will be in the middle of town.*

Gorsaf drenau
Train station
Mae **gorsaf drenau** *Caerdydd yn agos i'r siopau.*
Cardiff train station *is near to the shops.*

Gorsaf yr heddlu
Police station
Mae'r plismon yn gweithio yng **ngorsaf yr heddlu**.
The policeman works in the **police station**.

Grŵp *[eg]*
> grwpiau
Group
Bydd **grŵp** *o ddysgwyr yn mynd i'r theatr heno.*
A group *of learners will be going to the theatre tonight.*

Gwaith grŵp
Group work
Byddwn ni'n gwneud **gwaith grŵp** *am hanner awr.*
We will be doing **group work** *for half an hour.*

Gwaith *[eg]*
Work [noun] [See also > Gweithio]
Dyn ni'n dysgu Cymraeg yn y **gwaith**.
We are learning Welsh at **work**.
Ydy'r **gwaith** *yn talu am y cwrs?*
Is **work** *paying for the course?*

Gwaith cartre
Homework
Cofiwch wneud eich **gwaith cartre** *heno!*
Remember to do your **homework** *tonight!*

Gwallt *[eg]*
Hair
Mae **gwallt** *hir, du gyda hi.*
She's got long, black **hair**.

Gwanwyn *[eg]*
Spring
Mae'r **gwanwyn** *yn dod ar ôl y gaea.*
Spring *comes after winter.*

Gwddf *[eg]*   *Throat, neck [Standard Welsh]*
> gyddfau   *See >* **Llwnc**
Gweddol   *Rather, fairly + Treiglad Meddal*
                    Bydd hi'n **weddol** *dwym y prynhawn yma.*
                    It will be **fairly** *hot this afternoon.*
Gweithio   *To work*
                    Mae Gwen yn **gweithio** *fel nyrs yn Ysbyty*
                    Bronglais.
                    Gwen **works** *as a nurse at Bronglais Hospital.*
                    Dydy'r peiriant ddim yn **gweithio**.
                    The machine doesn't **work**.
Gweithiwr *[eg]* *Worker*
> gweithwyr   **Gweithiwr** *mewn ffatri yw Aled.*
                    Aled is a **worker** *in a factory.*
Gweld   *To see*
                    Dw i ddim wedi **gweld** *Megan ers wythnosau.*
                    I haven't **seen** *Megan for weeks.*
Gwely *[eg]*   *Bed*
> gwelyau   *Mae'r plentyn yn cysgu'n braf yn y* **gwely**.
                    The child is sleeping well/sound asleep in **bed**.
Gwener, dydd   *Friday*
                    Dw i'n hoffi **dydd Gwener** *– dw i'n gadael y*
                    gwaith yn gynnar.
                    I like **Friday** *– I leave work early.*

Nos Wener   *Friday night*
                   Maen nhw'n mynd ma's bob **nos Wener**.
                   They go out every **Friday night**.

Gwerthu   *To sell*
                    Dyn ni eisiau symud ond dyn ni ddim wedi
                    gwerthu'r *tŷ eto.*
                    We want to move but we haven't **sold** *the*
                    house yet.

Gwesty *[eg]*
> gwestai

Hotel

Byddwn ni'n aros mewn **gwesty** *ar ein gwyliau.*

We will be staying in a hotel on our holidays.

Gwin *[eg]*
> gwinoedd

Wine

Dw i'n cael pen tost ar ôl yfed **gwin** *coch.*

I get a headache after drinking red wine.

Gwir

(i) True

Ydy'r stori yma'n **wir**?

Is this story true?

(ii) Indeed

Wir *i chi!*

Absolutely! / Really! *[lit: Indeed to you]*

Gwisgo

To wear, dress

Mae'n rhaid i chi **wisgo** *eich cot – mae'n oer heddiw.*

You must wear your coat – it's cold today.

Gwlad *[eb]*
> gwledydd

Country

Mae Cymru'n **wlad** *fach.*

Wales is a small country.

Cefn gwlad

Countryside

Symudon nhw o Gaerdydd i **gefn gwlad** *Cymru.*

They moved from Cardiff to the Welsh countryside.

Gwlyb

Wet

Ar ôl y glaw, ro'n ni i gyd yn **wlyb** *iawn.*

After the rain, we were all very wet.

Gwneud

(i) To do

Dych chi wedi **gwneud** *yn dda yn y gwaith.*

You have done well at work.

(ii) To make

Bydda i'n **gwneud** *swper heno.*

I will be making dinner tonight.

Gŵr *[eg]*   *Husband*
> gwŷr   **Gŵr** *Mair yw Alun.*
    Alun is Mair's **husband.**

Gwraig *[eb]*   *Wife*
> gwragedd   **Gwraig** *Alun yw Mair.*
    Mair is Alun's **wife.**

Gŵr / Gwraig tŷ *House-husband / Housewife*
    Mae Glyn yn gwneud y gwaith tŷ – **gŵr tŷ** *yw e.*
    Glyn does the housework – he's a **house-husband.**
    Mae Sioned yn gwneud y gwaith tŷ – **gwraig tŷ** *yw hi.*
    Sioned does the housework – she's a **housewife.**

Gwrando (ar)   *To listen (to)*
    Bob bore, dw i'n **gwrando ar** *y radio.*
    Every morning, I **listen to** *the radio.*
    Beth ddwedoch chi? Do'n i ddim yn **gwrando.**
    What did you say? I wasn't **listening.**

Gwreiddiol   *Originally*
    Mae Anthony Hopkins yn dod o Fargam, Port Talbot, **yn wreiddiol.**
    Anthony Hopkins comes from Margam, Port Talbot, **originally.**

Gwrywaidd*   *Masculine (***Enw gwrywaidd** = *Masculine noun)*

Gwybod   *To know [a fact, something]*
    Dw i ddim yn **gwybod** *ble mae hi'n byw.*
    I don't **know** *where she lives.*

Gŵyl Dewi, dydd   *Saint David's day*
    Mae **dydd Gŵyl Dewi** *ar 1 Mawrth bob blwyddyn.*
    St David's day *is on 1 March every year.*

Gwyliau   *Holidays*
    Aethon ni i Sbaen ar ein **gwyliau.**
    We went to Spain on our **holidays.**

Gwylio
To view, to watch
*Wyt ti'n **gwylio** S4C?*
Do you watch S4C?

Gwyn
White
*Dw i'n yfed coffi **gwyn** gyda digon o laeth.*
I drink white coffee with enough / plenty of milk.

Gwynt *[eg]*
Wind
> gwyntoedd
*Mae **gwynt** y gogledd yn oer iawn.*
The north wind is very cold.

Gwyntog
Windy
*Roedd hi'n **wyntog** iawn neithiwr.*
It was very windy last night.

Gwyrdd
Green
*Mae hi'n hoffi bag **gwyrdd** ei ffrind.*
She likes her friend's green bag.

Gyda
(i) With
*Dewch **gyda** ni i'r dafarn!*
Come with us to the pub!
(ii) Used to form the 'have / got' construction in south Wales
*Mae dau o blant **gyda** Catrin.*
Catrin has got two children.
[lit: There are two children with Catrin]
*[See also: **Gan**]*

Gyferbyn (â)
Opposite
*Maen nhw'n byw **gyferbyn** â'r siopau.*
They live opposite the shops.

Gyrru
To drive
*Pwy sy'n **gyrru**'r car heno?*
Who's driving the car tonight?

Gyrrwr *[eg]*
Driver
> gyrwyr
Gyrrwr *tacsi yw Ffred.*
Ffred is a taxi driver.

H

Haf [eg]	*Summer*
	*Mae'r **haf** yn dod ar ôl y gwanwyn.*
	***Summer** comes after spring.*
Hala	*To send [Standard Welsh: **Anfon**]*
	*Maen nhw wedi **hala** siec yn y post.*
	*They have **sent** the cheque in the post.*
Hala at	*To send **to** [people]*
Halen [eg]	*Salt*
	*Mae gormod o **halen** yn ddrwg i chi.*
	*Too much **salt** is bad for you.*
	*Pupur a **halen**.*
	*Pepper and **salt**.*
Hamdden [eb]	*Leisure*
	*Beth dych chi'n wneud yn eich amser **hamdden**?*
	*What do you do in your **leisure** time?*
Hanner [eg]	*Half*
	*Bydda i'n cael **hanner** peint yn y dafarn heno.*
	*I'll be having **half** a pint in the pub tonight.*
	*Mae hi'n **hanner** awr wedi chwech.*
	*It's **half** past six.*
Hapus	*Happy*
	*Enillodd Gareth £5,000 [pum mil o bunnoedd] – roedd e'n **hapus** iawn!*
	*Gareth won £5,000 – he was very **happy**!*
Haul [eg]	*Sun*
	*Roedd hi'n braf gweld yr **haul** bob dydd yn Sbaen.*
	*It was lovely to see the **sun** every day in Spain.*
Heb	*Without + Treiglad Meddal*
	*Des i i'r dosbarth **heb** got y bore yma.*
	*I came to class **without** a coat this morning.*

Hedfan   *To fly*
*Byddwn ni'n **hedfan** o Heathrow i Las Vegas.*
We will be flying from Heathrow to Las Vegas.

Heddiw   *Today*
*Mae hi'n braf **heddiw** ond bydd hi'n wlyb fory.*
It's fine today but it will be wet tomorrow.

Heddlu *[eg]*   *Police*
*Ffoniwch 999 [naw naw naw] a gofynnwch
am yr **heddlu**.*
Phone 999 and ask for the police.

Hefyd   *Also, as well, too*
*Dych chi'n dod i'r dafarn **hefyd**?*
Are you coming to the pub as well/ too?

Help *[eg]*   *Help*
*Mae'r gwaith cartre'n anodd – dych chi'n
gallu rhoi **help** i fi?*
**The homework is difficult – can you give me
help** *[lit: give help to me]*?

Helpu   *To help*
*Bydd y tiwtor yn **helpu**'r dosbarth gyda'r
gwaith cartre.*
**The tutor will help the class with the
homework.**

Hen   *Old*
*Dydy 75 [saith deg pump] ddim yn **hen** y
dyddiau yma.*
75 isn't old these days.

Heno   *Tonight*
*Dw i ddim yn gallu mynd i'r gyngerdd **heno**.*
I can't go to the concert tonight.

Heol *[eb]*   *Road*
> heolydd   *Stopiodd y car yng nghanol yr **heol**.*
The car stopped in the middle of the road.

Het *[eb]*   *Hat*
> hetiau   *Gwisgwch **het** – mae hi'n oer iawn heddiw.*
              *Wear a **hat** – it's very cold today.*

Heulog   *Sunny*
              *Roedd hi'n **heulog** bob dydd ar ein gwyliau.*
              *It was **sunny** every day on our holidays.*

Hi   *(i) She*
              *Roedd **hi**'n chwarae pêl-droed.*
              ***She** was playing football.*
              (ii) her [ei]
              *Beth yw ei chyfeiriad **hi**?*
              *What is **her** address?*

Hir   *Long*
              *Mae'n ffordd **hir** i Madrid.*
              *It's a **long** way to Madrid.*

Hoci *[eg]*   *Hockey*
              *Doeddwn i ddim yn hoffi chwarae **hoci** yn yr ysgol.*
              *I didn't like playing **hockey** at school.*

Hoci iâ   Ice hockey
              Maen nhw'n chwarae hoci iâ yn Toronto.
              They play ice hockey in Toronto.

Hoffi   *To like*
              *Dw i'n **hoffi** pasta ond dw i ddim yn **hoffi** cyrri.*
              *I **like** pasta but I don't **like** curry.*

Hon   *This [feminine]*
              *Mae **hon** yn gêm dda.*
              ***This** is a good game.*
              *Siân yw **hon**...*
              ***This** is Siân...*

Honna   *That [feminine]*
              *... ac Elin yw **honna**.*
              *... and **that's** Elin.*

Hufen iâ *[eg]*   *Ice cream*
*Roedd hi'n braf bwyta **hufen iâ** yn yr haul.*
*It was lovely eating **ice cream** in the sun.*

Hwn   *This [masculine]*
*Tŷ mawr yw **hwn**.*
***This** is a big house.*
*Gareth yw **hwn**...*
***This** is Gareth...*

Hwnna / Hwnnw *That [masculine]*
*... ac Aled yw **hwnna**.*
*... and **that's** Aled.*

Hwyl *[eb]*   *Fun*
> hwyliau   *Cawson ni lawer o **hwyl** yn y dosbarth.*
*We had lots of **fun** in class.*

Pob hwyl   *All the best, goodbye*
Pob hwyl *i chi am y tro!*
***All the best** for the time being! / **Bye** for now!*

Hwyr   *Late*
*Mae hi bob amser yn cyrraedd yn **hwyr**.*
*She always arrives **late**.*

Hydref   *Autumn*
*Mae'r **hydref** yn dod ar ôl yr haf.*
***Autumn** comes after summer.*

Hydref *[mis]*   *October*
*Mis rhif deg yw mis **Hydref**.*
***October** is month number ten.*

Hyfryd   *Lovely, pleasant*
*Roedd yn **hyfryd** gweld Elwyn eto.*
*It was **lovely** to see Elwyn again.*

Hysbyseb *[eb]*   *Advert[isement]*
> hysbysebion   *Dw i ddim yn gwylio'r **hysbysebion** ar y teledu.*
*I don't watch the **adverts** on the television.*

I

I

(i) *To / For* + *Treiglad Meddal*
*Dyn ni'n mynd **i b**arti yn nhŷ Elin heno.*
**We're going to a party in Elin's house
tonight.**
*Beth dych chi'n mynd **i w**neud fory?*
What are you going to do tomorrow?
*Beth gest ti **i g**inio?*
What did you have for lunch?
(ii) *I / Me*
*Dw **i** wedi gorffen y gwaith erbyn hyn.*
I have finished the work by now.
*Rhowch yr arian **i f**i!*
**Give the money to me! / Give me the
money!**

I fyny
See > **Lan**

Up [Standard Welsh]

I ffwrdd
See > **Bant**

Away / Off [Standard Welsh]

I gyd

All [always comes after the noun]
*Mae'r plant **i gyd** yn siarad Cymraeg.*
All the children speak Welsh.

I lawr

Down
*Cerddon ni **i lawr** y mynydd.*
We walked down the mountain.
*Mae fy nghar wedi torri **i lawr**.*
My car has broken down.

Iau, dydd

Thursday
*Dw i'n mynd i siopa yn y dre bob **dydd Iau**.*
I go shopping in town every Thursday.

Nos Iau	*Thursday night*
	Maen nhw'n mynd i'r sinema **nos Iau**.
	They are going to the cinema on Thursday night.
Iawn	*(i) OK, alright*
	Ydy popeth yn **iawn**?
	Is everything OK / alright?
	(ii) Very [after the adjective]
	Yn y gaea, mae'r tŷ yma'n oer **iawn**.
	In the winter, this house is very cold.
Iechyd [eg]	*Health*
	Sut mae eich **iechyd** *chi erbyn hyn?*
	How is your health by now?
	Iechyd *da!*
	Good health! / Cheers!
Ifanc	*Young*
	Mae llawer o bobl **ifanc** *yn ein dosbarth ni.*
	There are many young people in our class.
Ionawr [mis]	*January*
	Mis **Ionawr** *yw mis cynta'r flwyddyn.*
	January is the first month of the year.

J

Jam [eg]	*Jam*
	Dw i eisiau brechdan **jam** *i de.*
	*I want a **jam** sandwich for tea.*

L

Lan	*Up* [Standard Welsh: **I fyny**]
	Maen nhw'n byw **lan** *ar y mynydd.*
	They live up *on the mountain.*
Ledled	*All over, across*
	Bydd y grŵp yn teithio **ledled** *Cymru.*
	The group will be travelling all over *Wales.*
Lemon *[eg]*	*Lemon*
> lemonau	*Maen nhw'n yfed te gyda* **lemon**.
	They're drinking tea with lemon.
Lico	*To like* [Other variant: **hoffi**]
	Dw i'n **lico** *pasta ond dw i ddim yn* **lico** *cyrri.*
	I like *pasta but I don't* **like** *curry.*
Lifft *[eg]*	*Lift*
> lifftiau	*(i) = in a building*
	Dydy'r **lifft** *ddim yn mynd yn gyflym iawn.*
	The lift *doesn't go very fast.*
	(ii) = ride
	Dych chi'n gallu rhoi **lifft** *i fi i'r dre?*
	Can you give me a lift *into town?*
Lolfa *[eb]*	*Lounge*
	Dw i'n edrych ar y teledu yn y **lolfa**.
	I'm watching television in the lounge.
Losin *[ell]*	*Sweets* [Other variants: **Taffis**]
	Dydy bwyta gormod o **losin** *ddim yn dda i'ch dannedd.*
	Eating too many sweets *is not good for your teeth.*

LL

Llaeth *[eg]*   *Milk*
*Dych chi'n cymryd **llaeth** yn eich te?*
Do you take milk in your tea?

Llaw *[eb]*   *Hand*
> dwylo   *Mae hi'n ysgrifennu gyda'r **llaw** dde.*
She writes with her right hand / she's right-handed.
*Golchwch eich **dwylo** cyn bwyta!*
Wash your hands before eating!

Llawer (o)   *Many, much, a lot [of], lots of*
*Mae **llawer** yn mynd ymlaen yma.*
There's a lot / much going on here.
*Bydd **llawer** o bobl yn y cyfarfod.*
There will be many / lots of people in the meeting.

Lle *[eg]*   *Place*
> lleoedd   *Mae'n **lle** da iawn i gael peint a siarad Cymraeg.*
It's a very good place to have a pint and speak Welsh.

Llenwi bylchau*   *Filling in the gaps*

Llestri *[ell]*   *Dishes*
*Pwy sy'n golchi'r **llestri** heno?*
Who's washing the dishes tonight?

Lliw *[eg]*   *Colour*
> lliwiau   *Beth yw **lliw** eich car chi?*
What's the colour of your car? / What colour is your car?

Lloegr *[eb]*   *England*
*Mae Birmingham a Windsor yn **Lloegr**.*
Birmingham and Windsor are in England.

Llun *[eg]* Picture
> lluniau *Beth yw gwaith y dyn yn y **llun**?*
  *What's the work of the man in the **picture**?/*
  *What does the man in the **picture** do?*

Llun, dydd Monday
  *Dw i'n mynd 'nôl i'r gwaith bob **dydd** Llun.*
  *I go back to work every **Monday**.*

Nos Lun Monday night
  *Dyn nhw ddim yn mynd ma's **nos Lun**.*
  *They don't go out on **Monday night**.*

Lluosog* Plural
Llwnc Throat *[Standard Welsh:* **Gwdd(f)***]*
  *Roedd **llwnc** tost gyda'r plant.*
  *The children had a sore **throat**.*

Llwyd Grey
  *Mae gwallt **llwyd** gyda Robyn.*
  *Robyn's got **grey** hair.*

Llyfr *[eg]* Book
> llyfrau *Dyn ni'n darllen **llyfr** da am Tom Jones.*
  *We're reading a good **book** about Tom Jones.*

Llyfr cwrs Course book
  *Dw i byth yn mynd i'r dosbarth heb fy **llyfr cwrs**.*
  *I never go to my class without my **course book**.*

Llygad *[eb]* Eye
> llygaid *Dyn ni'n gweld gyda'n **llygaid**.*
  *We see with our **eyes**.*

Llynedd (y) Last year
  *Y **llynedd**, aethon ni i Ffrainc ar ein gwyliau.*
  ***Last year**, we went to France on our holidays.*

Llysiau *[ell]* Vegetables
  *Dyn ni'n hoffi bwyta'r **llysiau** o'r ardd.*
  *We like eating the **vegetables** from the garden.*

Llysieuwr *[eg]* *Vegetarian (man)*
> llysieuwyr
Llysieuwraig *[eb]* *Vegetarian (woman)*
> llysieuwragedd **Llysieuwr** *ydy Twm: dydy o ddim yn bwyta*
cig.
Twm is a **vegetarian***: he doesn't eat meat.*
Llysieuwraig *ydy Myfanwy: dydy hi ddim*
yn bwyta cig.
Myfanwy is a **vegetarian***: she doesn't eat*
meat.
Llythyr *[eg]* *Letter (i.e. through the post)*
> llythyrau *Dych chi wedi cael y* **llythyr** *eto?*
Have you had the **letter** *yet?*

M

Mab *[eg]* *Son*
> meibion *Mae tri* **mab** *gyda fi ac maen nhw'n byw yn*
Llandrindod.
I have three **sons** *and they live in Llandrindod*
Wells.

Mab yng nghyfraith *Son-in-law*
Enw fy **mab yng nghyfraith** *(gŵr fy merch) yw Alun.*
My **son-in-law** *(my daughter's husband)'s name is*
Alun.

Maes parcio *[eg] Car park*
> meysydd parcio *Parcion ni ein car yn y* **maes parcio**.
We parked our car in the **car park**.
Mai *[mis]* *May*
Mis rhif pump yw mis **Mai**.
May *is month number five.*

Mam *[eb]* / **Mami** *Mother / Mami / Mum*

> mamau   *Mae hi'n byw gyda'i* **mam** *yng Nghastell-nedd.*
               She lives with her **mother** *in Neath.*
               Aeth **Mam** *i weld ei brawd yn y Rhyl.*
               Mam / Mum *went to see her brother in Rhyl.*

Mam yng nghyfraith *Mother-in-law*

               Enw fy **mam yng nghyfraith** *(mam fy ngwraig) yw*
               Gwyneth.
               My **mother-in-law** *(my wife's mother)'s name is Gwyneth.*

Mam-gu *[eb]*   *Grandmother / Gran / Nan*
               Mae fy **mam-gu**'*n dod o Hwlffordd yn*
               wreiddiol.
               My **grandmother** *comes from Haverfordwest*
               originally.
               Aeth **Mam-gu** *i weld ei chwaer yn y Fenni.*
               Gran / Nan *went to see her sister in*
               Abergavenny.

Hen fam-gu   *Great grandmother*
               Roedd fy **hen fam-gu**'*n siarad Cymraeg yn dda.*
               My **great grandmother** *spoke Welsh well.*

Ma's   *Out [Standard Welsh: (i)* **Allan***]*
               Rhaid i bawb fynd **ma's** *o'r neuadd.*
               Everyone has to go **out** *of the hall.*

Mawr   *Big, large*
               Enw fy mrawd **mawr** *yw Ifor.*
               The name of my **big** *brother is Ifor.*

Yn fawr   *A lot, a great deal, very much*
               Diolch **yn fawr** *iawn i chi.*
               Thank you **very much.**
               Dw i'n hoffi Pobol y Cwm **yn fawr.**
               I like Pobol y Cwm **a lot / a great deal / very much.**

Mawrth, dydd   *Tuesday*
*Dw i'n cwrdd â ffrindiau bob **dydd Mawrth**.*
*I meet friends every **Tuesday**.*

Nos Fawrth   *Tuesday night*
*Maen nhw'n mynd i'r ganolfan hamdden **nos Fawrth**.*
*They go to the leisure centre on **Tuesday night**.*

Mawrth *[mis]*   *March*
*Mis rhif tri yw mis **Mawrth**.*
March *is month number three.*

Medi *[mis]*   *September*
*Mis rhif naw yw mis **Medi**.*
September *is month number nine.*

Meddwl (am)   *To think [about]*
*Byddwn ni'n **meddwl** am ei syniad hi.*
*We will be **thinking** about her idea.*

Meddyg *[eg]*   *Doctor*
> meddygon   *Aeth Siôn at y **meddyg** ar ôl torri ei fraich.*
*Siôn went to the **doctor** after breaking his arm.*

Meddygfa *[eb]*   *Surgery, medical centre*
*Mae **meddygfa** Cwm Sgwt yn agor am wyth o'r gloch.*
*Cwm Sgwt **surgery** opens at eight o'clock.*

Mehefin *[mis]*   *June*
*Mis rhif chwech yw mis **Mehefin**.*
June *is month number six.*

Melyn   *Yellow*
*Roedd hi'n gyrru car **melyn**.*
*She was driving a **yellow** car.*

Menyn *[eg]*   *Butter*
*Maen nhw'n hoffi **menyn** ar eu bara.*
*They like **butter** on their bread.*

Menyw *[eb]* **Woman**
> menywod   *Pwy yw'r* **fenyw** *newydd yn y dosbarth?*
            Who is the new **woman** *in the class?*

Merch *[eb]* *(i) Daughter*
> merched   *Mae tair* **merch** *gyda fi ac maen nhw'n byw
             yn Wrecsam.*
             I have three **daughters** *and they live in
             Wrexham.*
             See > **Croten / Crotesi** *(ii) Girl [Standard
             Welsh]*

Merch yng nghyfraith *Daughter-in-law*
             Enw fy **merch yng nghyfraith** *(gwraig fy mab) yw Alys.*
             My **daughter-in-law** *(my son's wife)'s name is Alys.*

Mercher, dydd *Wednesday*
             Dw i'n aros yn y tŷ bob **dydd Mercher***.*
             I stay in the house every **Wednesday***.*

Nos Fercher *Wednesday night*
             Maen nhw'n chwarae tennis **nos Fercher***.*
             They play tennis on **Wednesday night***.*

Mewn   *In a*
             Maen nhw'n byw **mewn** *fflat yng nghanol y
             dre.*
             They live **in a** *flat in the middle of town.*

Mewn pryd   *In time*
             Cyrhaeddon ni'r ddrama **mewn pryd***.*
             We arrived at the play **in time***.*

Mis *[eg]* *Month*
> misoedd   *Maen nhw'n chwarae golff bob* **mis***.*
             They play golf every **month***.*

Modryb [eb] *Aunt / Auntie* [Also: **Anti**]
> modrybedd *Doedd fy **modryb** ddim yn gallu siarad Saesneg.*
  My auntie couldn't speak English.

Môr [eg] *Sea*
> moroedd *Mae hi'n rhy oer i nofio yn y **môr**.*
  It's too cold to swim in the sea.

Moron [ell] *Carrots*
  *Mae'r **moron** wedi dod o'n gardd ni.*
  The carrots have come from our garden.

Moyn *To want* [Standard Welsh: **Eisiau**]
  *Dw i'n **moyn** dysgu'r geiriau newydd.*
  I want to learn the new words.

Munud [eb] *Minute*
> munudau *Mae 60 [chwe deg] **munud** mewn awr.*
  There are 60 minutes in an hour.
  *Bydd y trên yn cyrraedd mewn pedair **munud**.*
  The train will be arriving in four minutes.

Mwy (o) *More* [Standard Welsh]
See > **Rhagor (o)**

Mwynhau *To enjoy*
  *Mae pawb yn **mwynhau**'r gyngerdd yn fawr.*
  Everybody is enjoying the concert a lot.

Mynd *To go*
  *Wyt ti'n **mynd** i'r sinema heno?*
  Are you going to the cinema tonight?
  *Dw i'n **mynd** i wneud y gwaith cartre heno.*
  I'm going to do the homework tonight.

Mynd am dro *To go for a walk*
  *Byddwn ni'n **mynd** am dro i'r parc ar ôl cinio.*
  We will be **going for a walk** in the park after lunch.

Mynd dros ben llestri *To go over the top, to go too far*
  *Dyna ddigon! Dych chi wedi **mynd** dros ben llestri.*
  That's enough! You've **gone over the top / gone too far.**

Mynd â

To take
Bydd Aled yn **mynd â** *chi yn ei gar.*
Aled will **take** *you in his car.*

Mynd â'r ci am dro

To take the dog for a walk
Dyn ni'n **mynd â'r ci am dro** *i'r traeth.*
We're **taking the dog for a walk** *to the beach.*

Mynydd *[eg]*
> mynyddoedd

Mountain
Dw i'n mynd i ddringo'r **mynydd** *fory.*
I'm going to climb the **mountain** *tomorrow.*

N

Nabod

To know [someone or somewhere]
Dych chi'n **nabod** *fy ngwraig, Mair?*
Do you **know** *my wife, Mair?*
Dw i wedi bod yn y Rhyl ond dw i ddim yn **nabod** *y lle'n dda.*
I've been in Rhyl but I don't **know** *the place well.*

Nadolig, y *[eg]*

Christmas
Nadolig *llawen a blwyddyn newydd dda i chi!*
Merry **Christmas** *and a happy new year to you!*
Mae'r **Nadolig** *ar 25 Rhagfyr bob blwyddyn.*
Christmas *is on 25 December every year.*

Nawr

Now
Dw i yn y dosbarth **nawr** *– wedyn bydda i'n mynd adre.*
I'm in class **now** *– then I'll be going home.*

Neb

Nobody, no one
*Does **neb** yn y tŷ ar hyn o bryd.*
There's nobody in the house at the moment.

Neges *[eb]*
> negeseuon

Message
*Mae hi wedi gadael **neges** ar eich peiriant ateb chi.*
She's left a message on your answer machine.

Anfon neges

To send a message
*Bydd y tiwtor yn **anfon neges** am y dosbarth nesa.*
The tutor will be **sending a message** about the next class.

Neges destun

Text message
*Ces i **neges destun** ar fy ffôn symudol.*
I got a **text message** on my mobile phone.

Neis

Nice
*Roedd y parti'n **neis** iawn – mwynhaodd pawb.*
The party was very **nice** – everyone enjoyed.

Neithiwr

Last night
Neithiwr *es i i'r dafarn ond heno dw i'n aros gartre.*
Last night I went to the pub but tonight I'm staying home.

Nesa

Next
*Bydd y dosbarth **nesa** ar ôl y Nadolig.*
The **next** class will be after Christmas.

Neu

Or + Treiglad Meddal
*Beth dych chi'n hoffi ei yfed: te **neu g**offi?*
What do you like drinking: tea **or** coffee?

Neuadd *[eb]*
> neuaddau

Hall
*Bydd cyngerdd y plant yn y **neuadd**.*
The children's concert will be in the **hall**.

Neuadd y dre	*Town hall*
	Daeth pawb i'r cyfarfod yn **neuadd y dre**.
	Everybody came to the meeting in the **town hall**.

Neuadd bentref *Village hall*
Mae Sadwrn Siarad yn **neuadd bentre** *Aberwylan.*
There's a Sadwrn Siarad in Aberwylan **village hall**.

Newid *To change*
Fyddwch chi'n **newid** *eich arian cyn y gwyliau?*
Will you be **changing** *your money before the holidays?*
Cyn mynd i'r theatr, mae e'n **newid** *ei ddillad.*
Before going to the theatre, he **changes** *his clothes.*

Newyddion [ell] *News*
Cawson ni **newyddion** *da: dyn ni wedi ennill car!*
We had some good **news**: *we've won a car!*
Dw i ddim yn hoffi gwylio'r **newyddion** *ar y teledu.*
I don't like watching the **news** *on the television.*

Nhw *(i) They*
Maen **nhw**'*n gwrando ar Radio Cymru bob bore.*
They *listen to Radio Cymru every morning.*
(ii) their [+ eu]
Beth yw eu cyfeiriad **nhw**?
What is **their** *address?*

Ni *(i) We*
Dyn **ni**'*n byw yng Nghaerdydd.*
We *live in Cardiff.*
(ii) our [+ ein]
Beth yw ein cyfeiriad **ni**?
What is **our** *address?*

Niwlog   *Misty / Foggy*
Dw i ddim yn gallu gweld llawer: mae hi'n **niwlog** *iawn.*
I can't see much: it's very **foggy.**

Nofio   *To swim*
Mae Aled yn mynd i **nofio** *o Aberystwyth i Bwllheli.*
Aled is going to **swim** *from Aberystwyth to Pwllheli.*

'Nôl   *See > Yn ôl*

Nos *[eb]*   *Night [i.e. as opposed to day or evening. See also > individual days of the week to say 'Monday night' etc.]*
Dw i ddim yn mynd ma's **nos** *fory.*
I'm not going out tomorrow **night.**

Noson *[eb]*   *Night / Evening [i.e. over a period of time / the events of the night or evening]*
Roedd neithiwr yn **noson** *dda iawn.* **Noson** *i'w chofio!*
Last night was a very good **night / evening.** *A* **night / evening** *to remember / to be remembered!*

Noswaith *[eb]*   *Evening (i.e. to refer to the time between day and night)*
Croeso i'r gyngerdd a **noswaith** *dda i chi i gyd.*
Welcome to the concert and good **evening** *to you all.*

Nyrs *[eb/eg]*   *Nurse*
> nyrsys
Nyrs *yn Ysbyty Gwynedd yw Siân.*
Siân's a **nurse** *at Ysbyty Gwynedd.*

Nyrsio   *To nurse*
Ers pryd mae Siân yn **nyrsio** *yn Ysbyty Gwynedd?*
Since when/how long has Siân been **nursing** *at Ysbyty Gwynedd?*

O

O	*Of / From* + *Treiglad Meddal* *Es i i'r siop i brynu peint **o** laeth.* *I went to the shop to buy a pint **of** milk.* *Mae Chris yn dod **o** Hirwaun yn wreiddiol.* *Chris comes **from** Hirwaun originally.*
O flaen	*In front of* *Maen nhw wedi gadael eu car **o flaen** y tŷ.* *They have left their car **in front of** the house.*
O gwbl	*At all* *Popeth yn iawn! Dim problem **o gwbl**!* *Everything's fine! No problem **at all**!*
O gwmpas	*Around* *Bydd y bws yn teithio **o gwmpas** Cymru.* *The bus will be travelling **around** Wales.*
O leia	*At least* *Bydd **o leia** hanner y dosbarth yn mynd i'r dafarn heno.* ***At least** half the class will be going to the pub tonight.*
O'r blaen	*Before (hand)* *Dw i ddim wedi gweld y bobl yma **o'r blaen**.* *I haven't seen these people **before**.*
O'r gloch	*O'clock* *Mae'r dosbarth yn dechrau am saith **o'r gloch**.* *The class begins at seven **o'clock**.*
Oed	*Age, [years] old* *Maen nhw'n 18 [un deg wyth] **oed** ac yn prynu cwrw yn y dafarn am y tro cynta.* *They're 18 **years old/aged** 18 and buying beer in the pub for the first time.* *Faint yw **oed** eich plant?* *How **old** are your children?*

Oer   *Cold*
*Fel arfer, mae'n **oer** iawn ym mis Ionawr.*
*Usually it's very **cold** in January.*

Oeri   *To get cold*
*Roedd hi'n braf iawn heddiw ond mae'n dechrau **oeri** nawr.*
*It was really lovely today but it's starting to **get cold** now.*

Ofnadwy   *Awful / Terrible*
*Roedd y tywydd yn **ofnadwy** – roedd hi'n bwrw glaw bob dydd.*
*The weather was **terrible/awful** – it was raining every day.*

Ond   *But*
*Mae Eleri'n dod i'r parti **ond** dydy Rachel ddim yn gallu dod.*
*Eleri's coming to the party **but** Rachel can't come.*

Opera sebon *[eb]*   *Soap opera*
> operâu sebon   **Opera sebon** *ar S4C yw* Pobol y Cwm.
Pobol y Cwm *is a **soap opera** on S4C.*

Oren   *Orange*
> orenau   *Dw i'n bwyta **oren** i frecwast bob bore.*
*I eat an **orange** for breakfast every morning.*
*Mae car **oren** gyda ni.*
*We've got an **orange** (coloured) car.*

Os   *If*
Os *dych chi'n barod, bant â chi!*
If *you're ready, off you go!*

Os gwelwch yn dda   *Please [formal or plural]*
*Agorwch y ffenest, **os gwelwch yn dda**.*
*Open the window, **please**.*

Os gweli di'n dda   *Please [informal and singular]*
*Agor y ffenest, **os gweli di'n dda**.*
*Open the window, **please**.*

P

Pa?
Which / What? + Treiglad Meddal
Pa ddiwrnod yw hi heddiw?
Which / What day is it today?

Pacio
To pack
Byddwn ni'n **pacio** ein bagiau ar ddiwedd y gwyliau.
*We will be **packing** our bags at the end of the holidays.*

Paent *[eg]*
*Paint [See also > **Peintio**]*
Dydy'r **paent** ddim yn sych eto.
*The **paint's** not dry yet.*

Pam?
Why?
Pam dych chi'n siarad Saesneg â fi?
Why are speaking English to me?

Pan
*When + Treiglad Meddal [use **Pryd?** to ask a question]*
Dewch i'r tŷ **pan f**yddwch chi'n barod.
*Come to the house **when** you are (you will be) ready.*

Paned *[eg]*
A cup of / A cuppa [Standard Welsh]
*See > **Dish[g]led***

Papur *[eg]*
> papurau
Paper
Does dim **papur** ysgrifennu gyda fi.
*I haven't got any writing **paper**.*

Papur newydd *[eg] Newspaper*
> papurau newydd Mae hi'n darllen y **papur newydd** ar ôl brecwast.
*She reads the **newspaper** after breakfast.*

Pâr *[eg]*
> parau*
Pair

Gwaith pâr*	*Work in pairs*
Para*	*To last*
Parc [eg]	*Park*
> parciau	*Es i â'r ci am dro i'r* **parc**.
	I took the dog for a walk to the park.
Parcio	*To park*
	Maen nhw wedi **parcio**'*r car o flaen y siop.*
	They have parked the car in front of the shop.
Parod	*Ready*
	Dych chi'n **barod** *i fynd ar y daith?*
	Are you ready to go on the trip?
	[Yn] **barod**, *bawb?*
	Ready everyone?
Parti [eg]	*Party*
> partïon	*Bydd y* **parti** *yn y neuadd am chwech o'r gloch.*
	The party will be in the hall at six o'clock.

Parti pen-blwydd [eg] **Birthday party**
Dw i'n rhy hen i gael **parti pen-blwydd!**
I'm too old to have a birthday party!

Partner [eg]	*Partner*
> partneriaid	*Gweithiwch gyda'ch* **partner** *am bum munud.*
	Work with your partner for five minutes.
	Dewch â ffrind neu **bartner** *i'r parti.*
	Bring a friend or partner to the party.
Pasg, y [eg]	*Easter*
	Does dim ysgol dros y **Pasg**.
	There's no school over Easter.
Pasta [eg]	*Pasta*
	Maen nhw'n bwyta **pasta** *yn yr Eidal.*
	They eat pasta in Italy.

Pawb	*Everybody / Everyone*
	Ydy **pawb** *yn gallu dod i'r dosbarth yr wythnos nesa?*
	Can everyone / everybody *come to the class next week?*
	Da iawn, **pawb** *– unwaith eto!*
	Well done everyone *– once again!*
Peidio (â)	*To not do something*
	Peidiwch *â siarad Saesneg yn y dosbarth!*
	Don't / Do not *speak English in class!*
Peint *[eg]*	*Pint*
	Bydda i'n cael **peint** *(o gwrw) yn y dafarn heno.*
	I'll be having a **pint** *(of beer) in the pub tonight.*
Peintio	*To paint*
	Byddwn ni'n **peintio**'*r stafell yn felyn.*
	We will be **painting** *the room yellow.*
Peiriant *[eg]*	*Machine*
> peiriannau	*Dydy'r* **peiriant** *ddim yn gweithio: mae e wedi torri.*
	The **machine** *isn't working: it's broken.*

Peiriant ateb	*Answer machine/phone*
	Gadewch neges ar y peiriant ateb.
	Leave a message on the **answer machine**.
Peiriant CD	*CD machine*
	Gwrandewch ar y canu ar y peiriant CD.
	Listen to the singing on the **CD machine**.
Peiriant DVD	*DVD machine*
	Gwyliwch y ffilm ar y peiriant DVD.
	Watch the film on the **DVD machine**.
Peiriant golchi	*Washing machine*
	Rhowch eich dillad yn y peiriant golchi.
	Put your clothes in the **washing machine**.

Peiriant golchi llestri *Dishwasher*

Ar ôl bwyd, rhowch bopeth yn y **peiriant golchi llestri**.
After food, put everything in the **dishwasher**.

Pêl *[eb]*   *Ball*
> peli   *Mae'r* **bêl** *wedi mynd i ardd drws nesa.*
                   The ball *has gone into next door's garden.*

Pêl-droed *[eg]*   *Football*
                   Roedd y plant yn chwarae **pêl-droed** *ar y stryd.*
                   The children were playing **football** *on the street.*

Pell   *Far*
                   Mae America'n **bell** *o Gymru.*
                   America is **far** *from Wales.*

Pen *[eg]*   *Head*
> pennau   *Gwisgwch het i gadw eich* **pen** *yn sych.*
                   Wear a hat to keep your **head** *dry.*

Pen tost   *Headache*
                   Roedd y canu'n ofnadwy – roedd **pen tost** *gyda fi!*
                   The singing was awful – I had a **headache**!

Pen-blwydd *[eg]* *Birthday*
                   21 [dau ddeg un] oed heddiw?
                   Pen-blwydd *hapus i ti!*
                   21 today? Happy **birthday** *to you!*

Pennaeth *[eg]*   *Head [Also in school context:* **Prifathro / Prifathrawes** *– Headmaster / Headmistress]*

Mae'r **pennaeth** *newydd eisiau newid popeth yn yr ysgol.*
The new head *wants to change everything in the school.*

Pensil *[eg]* *Pencil*
> pensiliau   *Mae* **pensil** *gyda hi ac mae hi'n barod i ysgrifennu.*
She's got a **pencil** *and she's ready to write.*

Pentre *[eg]* *Village*
> pentrefi   *Dyn ni'n byw mewn* **pentre** *bach yn y wlad.*
We live in a small **village** *in the country.*

Penwythnos *[eg]* *Weekend*
> penwythnosau *Fydda i ddim yn gweithio dros y* **penwythnos**.
I won't be working over the **weekend**.

Person *[eg]* *Person*
> pobl/personau *Dych chi'n nabod y* **person** *newydd yn y dosbarth?*
Do you know the new **person** *in class?*

Pert   *Pretty, cute*
Mae babi bach **pert** *gyda nhw.*
They've got a **pretty/cute** *little baby.*
Roedd y ferch yn edrych yn **bert** *yn ei het newydd.*
The girl looked **pretty** *in her new hat.*

Peswch *[eg]* *Cough*
Mae e'n smygu gormod ac mae **peswch** *arno fe nawr.*
He smokes too much and he's got a **cough** *now.*

Peth *[eg]* *Thing*
> pethau   *Beth yw enw'r* **peth** *yna yn Gymraeg?*
What's the name of that **thing** *in Welsh?*
Dyna'r **peth** *pwysig.*
That's the **important** *thing.*

Plentyn *[eg]* *Child*
> plant
Fel **plentyn***, ro'n i'n mynd i ysgol Gymraeg.*
As a child*, I went to a Welsh-medium school.*
Mae pedwar **plentyn** *gyda fi / Mae pedwar o* **blant** *gyda fi.*
I've got four **children**.

Plismon *[eg]* *Policeman*
> plismyn
Plismon *yw Marc – mae e'n gweithio gyda Heddlu Gwent.*
Marc is a **policeman** *– he works with Gwent Police*

Plismones *[eb]* *Policewoman*
> plismonesau
Plismones *yw Elen – mae hi'n gweithio gyda Heddlu Gogledd Cymru.*
Elen is a **policewoman** *– she works with North Wales Police.*

Pob *Each / Every*
Erbyn hyn, mae **pob** *dysgwr yn siarad Cymraeg yn gynta.*
By now, every **learner** *speaks Welsh first.*

Pob un *Each/every one*
Bydd **pob un** *o'r plant yn canu yn y gyngerdd.*
Every/each one *of the children will be singing in the concert.*

Pobl *[eb]* *People*
Mae **pobl** *yn gyrru ar y dde yn Ffrainc.*
People *drive on the right in France.*

Pont *[eb]* *Bridge*
> pontydd
Gyrron ni dros **Bont** *Hafren, o Gymru i Loegr.*
We drove over the Severn **Bridge***, from Wales to England.*

Popeth   *Everything*
*Erbyn hyn, dw i'n deall **popeth** yn y dosbarth.*
By now, I understand everything in class.
Popeth *yn iawn!*
Everything's OK / fine!

Porc *[eg]*   *Pork*
*Cawson ni **borc** i ginio dydd Sul.*
We had pork for Sunday lunch.

Post *[eg]*   *Post*
*Mae'r llythyr yn y **post**.*
The letter's in the post.

Postio   *To post*
***Postiais** i'r llythyr ddoe.*
I posted the letter yesterday.

Postmon *[eg]*   *Postman*
> postmyn   *Bydd y **postmon** yn dod â'r llythyr fory.*
**The postman will be bringing the letter
tomorrow.**

Potel *[eb]*   *Bottle*
> poteli   *Mae hi'n yfed **potel** o laeth bob dydd.*
She drinks a bottle of milk every day.

Priod, yn briod *Married*
*Mae Liz a Richard **yn briod** ers blwyddyn
nawr.*
**Liz and Richard have been married for a
year now.**

Pris *[eg]*   *Price*
> prisiau   *Beth yw **pris** y tocyn?*
What's the price of the ticket?

Problem *[eb]*   *Problem*
> problemau   *Dim **problem** o gwbl!*
No problem at all!

Pryd?   *When [to ask a question]?*
***Pryd** mae'r ddrama'n dechrau?*
When is the play starting?

Prynu *To buy*
Dych chi wedi **prynu** *eich anrhegion Nadolig eto?*
Have you **bought** *your Christmas presents yet?*

Prysur *Busy*
Mae'r siopau'n **brysur** *iawn dros y Nadolig.*
The shops are very **busy** *over Christmas.*

Punt *[eb]* *Pound [£]*
> punnoedd/punnau *Pris y llyfr yw pum* **punt.**
The price of the book is five **pounds.**

Pupur *[eg]* *Pepper*
Roedd y **pupur** *yn dwym iawn.*
The **pepper** *was very hot.*
Pupur *a halen.*
Pepper *and salt.*

Pwdin *[eg]* *Pudding*
> pwdinau *Does neb eisiau* **pwdin** *ar ôl cinio.*
Nobody wants **pudding** *after lunch.*

Pwll nofio *[eg]* *Swimming pool*
> pyllau nofio *Oes* **pwll nofio** *yn y ganolfan hamdden?*
Is there a **swimming pool** *in the leisure centre?*

Pwy? *Who?*
Pwy *dych chi?*
Who *are you?*
Pwy *yw tiwtor y dosbarth?*
Who *is the class tutor?*
Pwy *sy'n dod i'r dafarn gyda chi?*
Who *is coming to the pub with you?*

Pwysig *Important*
Mae'n **bwysig** *siarad Cymraeg bob tro.*
It's **important** *to speak Welsh every time.*

Pys *[ell]*   *Peas*
Dw i'n hoffi bwyta porc, **pys** *a sglodion.*
I like eating pork,* peas *and chips.

Pysgodyn *[eg]*   *Fish*
> pysgod   *Enw'r* **pysgodyn** *yw Nemo.*
The* fish *is called Nemo.
Mae digon o **bysgod** *yn y môr.*
There are enough / plenty of* fish *in the sea.

Pysgodyn aur   Goldfish
Dw i wedi ennill **pysgodyn aur***!*
**I've won a goldfish*!*

R

Radio *[eg]*   *Radio*
Dw i'n gwrando ar y **radio** *yn y car.*
I listen to the* radio *in the car.

Rygbi *[eg]*   *Rugby*
Roedd Gareth yn chwarae **rygbi** *yn y parc ddoe.*
Gareth was playing* rugby *in the park yesterday.

RH

Rhagfyr *[mis]*   *December*
Mis rhif un deg dau yw mis **Rhagfyr**.
***December* is month number twelve.**

Rhaglen *[eb]*   *Programme*
> rhaglenni   *Roedd enwau'r actorion yn y* **rhaglen**.
***The names of the actors were in the* programme.**

Dyn ni'n mwynhau'r **rhaglenni** *ar S4C.*
We enjoy the programmes on S4C.

Rhagor (o) *More [Standard Welsh: Mwy (o)]*
Dych chi eisiau **rhagor o** *siwgr?*
Do you want more sugar?

Rhaid *[eg]* *Necessity > used to say you 'must' do something*
Mae'n **rhaid** *i bawb siarad Cymraeg yn y dosbarth.*
Everyone must speak Welsh in class.

Rhain (y) *These*
Fy llyfrau i yw'r **rhain.**
These are my books.

Rheina (y) *Those*
Dy lyfrau di yw'r **rheina.**
Those are your books.

Rhedeg *To run*
Roedd Guto Nyth Brân yn gallu **rhedeg** *yn gyflym iawn.*
Guto Nyth Brân could run very quickly.

Rhiant *[eg]* *Parent/s*
> rhieni *Mae croeso i bob* **rhiant** *yn yr ysgol newydd.*
Every parent is welcome in the new school.
Bydd noson **rieni** *yn yr ysgol heno.*
There will be a parents' evening in the school tonight.

Rhif *[eg]* *Number [= numeral]*
> rhifau *Dw i wedi ennill y bingo! Dyma fy* **rhifau** *i.*
I've won the bingo! Here are my numbers.

Rhoi *(i) To give*
Wyt ti wedi **rhoi'r** *anrheg ben-blwydd i Siân?*
Have you given Siân the birthday present / given the birthday present to Siân?
(ii) To put
See > **Dodi**

Rhwng	*Between*
	*Mae Llandudno **rhwng** Bangor a Wrecsam.*
	*Llandudno is **between** Bangor and Wrexham.*
Rhy	*Too* + *Treiglad Meddal*
	Dw i ddim yn gallu yfed y te yma. Mae'n
	***rhy d**wym.*
	*I can't drink this tea. It's **too** hot.*
Rhywbeth	*Something*
	*Roedd **rhywbeth** i bawb yn y sioe.*
	*There was **something** for everyone in the show.*
Rhywun	*Someone / Somebody*
	*Mae **rhywun** wrth y drws – pwy?*
	*There's **someone** at the door – who?*

S

Sadwrn, dydd	*Saturday*
	*Dw i'n mynd i wylio rygbi bob **dydd Sadwrn**.*
	*I go to watch rugby every **Saturday**.*
Nos Sadwrn	*Saturday night*
	*Maen nhw'n mynd ma's i'r dre **nos Sadwrn**.*
	*They are going out to town on **Saturday night**.*
Sadwrn Siarad	*A Saturday all-day course with emphasis on speaking Welsh*
Saesneg	*(i) English (language) [adjective]*
	*Rhaglen **Saesneg** yw Coronation Street.*
	*Coronation Street is an **English (language)** programme.*
	(ii) English language [noun]
	*Does neb yn siarad **Saesneg** yn y dosbarth.*
	*Nobody speaks **English** in class.*

Sais *[eg]*   *An Englishman*
Saesnes *[eb]*   *An English woman*
> Saeson   *The English*

Sais *yw Reginald – mae e'n dod o Leeds yn wreiddiol.*

Reginald is **English** *(i.e. an Englishman) – he comes from Leeds originally.*

Saesnes *yw Pippa – mae hi'n dod o Windsor yn wreiddiol.*

Pippa is **English** *(i.e. an English woman) – she comes from Windsor originally.*

Sâl   *Ill [Standard Welsh]*

See > **Tost**

Salad *[eg]*   *Salad*
> saladau   *Dyn ni'n hoffi bwyta* **salad** *yn yr haf.*

We like eating **salad** *in the summer.*

Sawl?   *How many? [Standard Welsh:* **Faint***]*

Sawl *plentyn sy yn y dosbarth?*

How many *children are in the class?*

Sbaen *[eb]*   *Spain*

Mae Madrid a Málaga yn **Sbaen**.

Madrid and Málaga are in **Spain**.

Sbectol *[eb]* *Glasses*

Mae'n rhaid i fi wisgo **sbectol** *i ddarllen.*

I have to wear **glasses** *to read.*

Sgio   *To ski, go skiing*

Dyn ni'n mynd i **sgio** *yn Aviemore ym mis Chwefror.*

We're **going skiing** *in Aviemore in February.*

Sglodion *[ell]* *Chips*

Maen nhw'n bwyta **sglodion** *gyda popeth!*

They eat **chips** *with everything!*

Sgrifennu *See >* **Ysgrifennu**
Sgwennu   *See >* **Ysgrifennu**
Sgwrs *[eb]*   *Chat, conversation*

> sgyrsiau *Dw i'n mwynhau* **sgwrs** *fach yn Gymraeg.*
I enjoy a little chat in Welsh.

Siaced *[eb]* *Jacket*
> siacedi *Mae Siôn wedi gadael ei* **siaced** *yn y dafarn.*
Siôn has left his jacket in the pub.

Siarad (â) *To speak, talk [to]*
Dych chi'n **siarad** *Cymraeg?*
Do you speak Welsh?
Dw i'n **siarad** *Cymraeg* **â** *nhw bob tro.*
I always talk to them in Welsh.

Sigarét *[eb]* *Cigarette*
> sigaréts *Maen nhw o flaen y dafarn yn smygu* **sigarét.**
They are in front of the pub smoking a cigarette.

Sillafu *To spell*
Sut dych chi'n **sillafu**'*r gair 'cyfarwyddiadau'?*
How do you spell the word 'cyfarwyddiadau'?

Sinema *[eb]* *Cinema*
> sinemâu *Pa ffilm weloch chi yn y* **sinema** *neithiwr?*
Which film did you see in the cinema last night?

Siocled *[eg]* *Chocolate*
> siocledi *Ar ôl bwyta gormod o* **siocled,** *roedd hi'n dost.*
After eating too much chocolate, she was ill.

Siocled /poeth *Hot chocolate*
Cyn mynd i'r gwely, dw i'n yfed **siocled poeth.**
Before going to bed, I drink hot chocolate.

Sioe *[eb]* *Show*
> sioeau *Bydd llawer o bobl enwog yn y* **sioe** *eleni.*
There will be many famous people in the show this year.

Siôn Corn *[eg]* *Father Christmas*

92

Mae **Siôn Corn** *yn galw bob Nadolig.*
Father Christmas *calls every Christmas.*

Siop *[eb]*
> siopau

Shop
Dydy'r **siop** *ddim yn agor ddydd Sul.*
The shop *doesn't open on Sunday.*

Siop bapurau
Paper shop / Newsagents
Maen nhw'n gwerthu papurau yn y **siop bapurau**.
They sell papers in the newsagents / paper shop.

Siop ddillad
Clothes shop
Maen nhw'n gwerthu dillad yn y **siop ddillad**.
They sell clothes in the clothes shop.

Siop fara
Bread shop / Baker's
Maen nhw'n gwerthu bara yn y **siop fara**.
They sell bread in the baker's / bread shop.

Siop fwyd
Food shop
Maen nhw'n gwerthu bwyd yn y **siop fwyd**.
They sell food in the food shop.

Siop lyfrau
Book shop
Maen nhw'n gwerthu llyfrau yn y **siop lyfrau**.
They sell books in the book shop.

Siop sglodion
Chip shop
Maen nhw'n gwerthu sglodion yn y **siop sglodion**.
They sell chips in the chip shop.

Siopa
To shop
Dyn ni'n **siopa** *am fwyd unwaith yr wythnos.*
We shop *for food once a week.*

Siopwr *[eg]*
> siopwyr

(i) Shopper
Roedd llawer o **siopwyr** *yn y dre cyn y Nadolig.*
There were many shoppers *in town before Christmas.*

(ii) Shopkeeper

*Prynodd y **siopwr** y siop yn 2012.*

The shopkeeper bought the shop in 2012.

Siwgr *[eg]*   Sugar

*Dw i ddim yn hoffi **siwgr** mewn coffi.*

I don't like sugar in coffee.

Siŵr   Sure, certain

*Dyn ni ddim yn **siŵr** pryd bydd e'n cyrraedd.*

We aren't sure when he'll be arriving.

Siŵr o fod   Probably

*Bydd e'n cyrraedd yn hwyr, **siŵr o fod**.*

He will probably be arriving late.

Smwddio   To iron, do the ironing

*Mae'n rhaid i chi **smwddio** eich dillad cyn mynd ma's.*

You must iron your clothes before going out.

Smygu [Ysmygu] *To smoke*

*Does dim **smygu** yn y tafarnau yng Nghymru.*

There's no smoking in the pubs in Wales.

Stadiwm *[eg]*   Stadium

*Byddan nhw'n chwarae yn y **stadiwm** newydd.*

They will be playing the new stadium.

Stafell *[eb]*   Room *[in a building]*
> stafelloedd

*Mae'r dosbarth mewn **stafell** fawr.*

The class is in a big room.

Stafell fwyta   Dining room
> stafelloedd bwyta   *Bydd swper yn y **stafell fwyta**.*
   Dinner will be in the dining room.

Stafell fyw   Living room
> stafelloedd byw   *Dyn ni'n edrych ar y teledu yn y **stafell fyw**.*
   We watch television in the living room.

Stafell wely
> stafelloedd gwely

Bedroom
Maen nhw eisiau prynu tŷ gyda phedair **stafell wely**.
They want to buy a house with four **bedrooms**.

Stafell ymolchi
> stafelloedd ymolchi

Bathroom
Dw i'n mynd i gael bath yn y **stafell ymolchi**.
I'm going to have a bath in the **bathroom**.

Stopio

To stop
Dyna ddigon – **stopiwch** *nawr!*
That's enough – **stop** *now!*

Stori [eb]
> storïau
Also used is
> straeon

Story
Does dim digon o amser nawr – mae hi'n **stori** *hir.*
There's not enough time now – it's a long **story**.
Roedd y plant yn mwynhau amser **stori**.
The children used to enjoy **story** *time.*

Stormus

Stormy
Bydd hi'n noson **stormus** *heno, gyda llawer o wynt a glaw.*
It'll be a **stormy** *night tonight, with a lot of wind and rain.*

Stryd [eb]
> strydoedd

Street
Does neb arall yn byw yn ein **stryd** *ni.*
Nobody else lives in our **street**.

Stryd fawr

High street
Mae llawer o siopau'r **stryd fawr** *wedi cau.*
Many of the **high street** *shops have closed.*

Sudd [eg]

Juice
Dw i'n yfed **sudd** *oren / afal i frecwast.*
I drink orange / apple **juice** *for breakfast.*

Sul, dydd	*Sunday*
	*Dw i byth yn gweithio ar **ddydd** Sul.*
	*I never work on **Sunday(s)**.*
Nos Sul	*Sunday night*
	*Maen nhw'n mynd i'r gwely'n gynnar ar **nos** Sul.*
	*They go to bed early on **Sunday night(s)**.*
Sut?	*How? [Other variant: shwt]*
	*Sut dych chi? / **Shwt** dych chi?*
	***How** are you?*
	*Sut/**Shwt** dych chi'n dweud 'how' yn Gymraeg?*
	***How** do you say 'how' in Welsh?*
Swper [eg]	*Supper*
> swperau	*Am faint o'r gloch mae **swper** heno?*
	*What time is **supper** tonight?*
Swyddfa [eb]	*Office*
> swyddfeydd	*Dyn ni'n gweithio mewn **swyddfa** yng nghanol y dre.*
	*We work in an **office** in the centre of town.*
Swyddfa bost	*Post office*
> swyddfeydd post	*Mae hi wedi mynd i'r **swyddfa bost** i bostio llythyr.*
	*She has gone to the **post office** to post a letter.*
Sych	*Dry*
	*Fory, bydd hi'n braf ac yn **sych**.*
	*Tomorrow, it will be fine and **dry**.*
Syched	*Thirsty (lit: thirst)*
	*Maen nhw'n prynu potel o ddŵr. Mae **syched** arnyn nhw.*
	*They're buying a bottle of water. They're **thirsty** / There's a **thirst** on them.*
Symud	*To move*
	*Mae'r dosbarth wedi **symud** o'r neuadd i'r ysgol.*
	*The class has **moved** from the hall to the school.*

Symud (tŷ)   *To move (house)*
                         Symudon *ni o Aberystwyth i Gaerfyrddin.*
                         We **moved** *from Aberystwyth to Carmarthen.*

Syniad *[eg]*   *Idea*
> syniadau   *Mae e'n* **syniad** *da.*
                         It's a good **idea.**
                         Does dim **syniad** *gyda fi.*
                         I have no **idea.**

Syth   *Straight*
                         Bydda i'n mynd yn **syth** *i'r dobsarth heno.*
                         I will be going **straight** *to class tonight.*

Syth ymlaen   *Straight on* *[directions]*
                         Trowch i'r dde, yna ewch yn **syth ymlaen.**
                         Turn to the right, then go **straight on.**

T

Tabled *[eb]*   *Tablet*
> tabledi   *Os oes pen tost gyda chi, mae'n rhaid i chi*
                         gymryd **tabled.**
                         If you've got a headache, you must take a **tablet.**

Tacsi *[eg]*   *Taxi*
> tacsis   *Es i adre o'r dafarn mewn* **tacsi.**
                         I went home from the pub in a **taxi.**

Tachwedd *[mis]*   *November*
                         Mis rhif un deg un yw mis **Tachwedd.**
                         November *is month number eleven.*

Tad *[eg]* / **Dad** / **Dadi** *Father / Dad / Daddy*
> tadau   *Mae* **tad** *Ffion yn byw yng Nglyn Ebwy.*
                         Ffion's **father** *lives in Ebbw Vale.*
                         Aeth **Dad** *i weld ei ffrind yng Nghaergybi.*
                         Dad *went to see his friend in Holyhead.*

Tad yng nghyfraith *Father-in-law*
*Enw fy **nhad yng nghyfraith** (tad fy ngŵr) yw Gareth.*
*My **father-in-law** (my husband's father)'s name is Gareth.*

Tad-cu *[eg]* *Grandfather / Grandpa / Grampy*
*Mae fy **nhad-cu**'n dod o Abergwaun yn wreiddiol.*
My grandfather *comes from Fishguard originally.*
*Aeth **Tad-cu** i weld ei chwaer ym Mhrestatyn.*
Grandpa / Grampy *went to see his sister in Prestatyn.*

Hen dad-cu *Great grandfather*
*Roedd fy **hen dad-cu**'n siarad Cymraeg yn dda.*
*My **great grandfather** spoke Welsh well.*

Tafarn *[eb]* *Pub, tavern*
> tafarnau *Dych chi eisiau dod i'r **dafarn** gyda ni?*
*Do you want to come to the **pub** with us?*

Taflen *[eb]* *Leaflet, handout, sheet*
> taflenni *Ysgrifennwch yr atebion ar y **daflen**.*
*Write the answers on the **sheet**.*

Taflen waith *[eb]* *Worksheet*
> taflenni gwaith *Gwnewch y **daflen waith** erbyn yr wythnos nesa.*
*Do the **worksheet** by next week.*

Taith *[eb]* *Trip, journey [See also > **Teithio**]*
> teithiau *Mae'r **daith** o Abertawe i Fangor yn hir.*
*The **journey/trip** from Swansea to Bangor is long.*

Tal *Tall*
*Mae Ifan yn **dal**.*
*Ifan is **tall**.*

Talu + am
To pay (a bill etc) + for
*Dych chi wedi **talu** am y bwyd eto?*
Have you paid for the food yet?

Tan
Until + Treiglad Meddal
*Byddwn ni'n aros **tan dd**ydd Llun nesa.*
We will be staying until next Monday.

Tân *[eg]*
> tanau
Fire
*Eisteddon ni o flaen y **tân** yn y dafarn.*
We sat in front of the fire in the pub.

Ar dân
On fire
*Rhedwch! Mae'r tŷ **ar dân**!*
*Run! The house is **on fire**!*

Tatws *[ell]*
Potatoes
*Maen nhw'n gwneud sglodion o'r **tatws**.*
They're making chips from the potatoes.

Te *[eg]*
Tea (i) drink
*Dw i'n yfed paned o **de** bob bore.*
I drink a cup of tea every morning.
Tea (ii) mealtime
*Beth sy i **de** heno?*
What's for tea tonight?

Tedi *[eg]*
> tedis
Teddy
*Aeth y plentyn â'r **tedi** i'r ysgol.*
The child took the teddy to school.

Tegan *[eg]*
> teganau
Toy
*Mae'r plant yn chwarae gyda eu **teganau**.*
The children are playing with their toys.

Teimlo
To feel
*Dw i ddim yn **teimlo**'n dda – dw i'n mynd adre.*
I don't feel well – I'm going home.

Teisen *[eb]*
> teisennau

Cake

Prynon ni **deisen** *siocled fawr ar ei phen-blwydd hi.*

We bought a big chocolate **cake** *on her birthday.*

[See also > **Cacen***]*

Teithio

To travel

Bydda i'n **teithio** *i Ffrainc fory.*

I'll be **travelling** *to France tomorrow.*

Teledu *[eg]*

Television / TV

Beth sy ar y **teledu** *heno?*

What's on **television / TV** *tonight?*

Tennis *[eg]*

Tennis

Dyn ni'n chwarae **tennis** *yn y ganolfan hamdden.*

We play **tennis** *in the leisure centre.*

Teulu *[eg]*

Family

Mae **teulu** *mawr gyda ni.*

We have a large **family***.*

Oes **teulu** *gyda chi yng Nghymru?*

Do you have **family** *in Wales?*

Ti / di

(i) You [informal singular]

Helo, Aled. Sut / shwt wyt **ti** *heddiw?*

Hello, Aled. How are **you** *today?*

Siwan, wyt **ti***'n barod?*

Siwan, are **you** *ready?*

(ii) Your [+ **dy***]*

Ydy dy blant **di***'n mynd i ysgol Gymraeg?*

Do **your** *children go to a Welsh (language) school?*

Tîm *[eg]*
> timau

Team

Dw i'n chwarae yn y **tîm** *pêl-droed.*

I play in the football **team***.*

Tipyn (o)
A bit [of] / a little
Mae Glasgow yn bell. Mae **tipyn** *o ffordd i fynd eto!*
Glasgow's far. There's a **bit of** *a way to go yet!*

Tipyn bach
A little bit
Paned o de a **thipyn bach** *o laeth, os gwelwch yn dda.*
A cup of tea and **a little bit (drop)** *of milk please.*

Tiwtor *[eg]*
> tiwtoriaid
Tutor
Mae'r **tiwtor** *yma'n dysgu'r dosbarth nos Lun.*
This **tutor** *teaches the class on Monday night.*

Tocyn *[eg]*
> tocynnau
Ticket
Dyn ni'n mynd i brynu **tocyn** *i'r gêm.*
We're going to buy a **ticket** *for the game.*

Torri
To break
Ydy'r ffenest wedi **torri**?
Has the window **broken**?
Mae'r car wedi **torri** *i lawr.*
The car has **broken** *down.*

Tost *[eg]*
Toast
Dw i'n hoffi bwyta **tost** *a jam i frecwast.*
I like eating **toast** *and jam for breakfast.*

Tost
Ill [Standard Welsh: **Sâl**]
Dydy hi ddim yn y gwaith heddiw – mae hi'n **dost**.
She's not in work today – she's **ill**.

Traeth *[eg]*
> traethau
Beach
Yn yr haf, dyn ni'n mynd i'r **traeth** *bob dydd.*
In the summer, we go to the **beach** *every day.*

Tre[f] *[eb]*
> trefi
Town
Tre *fach hyfryd yw Dinbych.*
Denbigh's a lovely little **town**.

Treiglad*	***Mutation***
	*Treiglad Meddal** *Soft Mutation*
	*Treiglad Llaes** *Aspirate Mutation*
	*Treiglad Trwynol** *Nasal Mutation*

Trên *[eg]*
> trenau

Train
*Bydd y **trên** nesa yn gadael am un o'r gloch.*
The next train will be leaving at one o'clock.

Trist

Sad
*Cawson ni newyddion **trist** y bore yma.*
We had some sad news this morning.

Tro *[eg]*
> troeon

*Turn [See also > **Mynd** > **Mynd am dro**]*
*Eich **tro** chi yw hi nawr.*
It's your turn now.

Bob tro

Every time
Bob tro *dw i'n gweld Siân, mae hi'n siarad Cymraeg â fi.*
Every time *I see Siân, she speaks Welsh to me.*

Troed *[eb]*
> traed

Foot
*Rhowch eich **troed** yn y dŵr!*
Put your foot in the water!

Troi

To turn
*Dych chi'n **troi** i'r dde ar ôl y capel.*
You turn to the right after the chapel.
Trowch *i dudalen 10 [deg], os gwelwch yn dda!*
Turn to page 10, please!

Trwy

Through + Treiglad Meddal
*Bydda i'n gyrru **trwy g**anol y dre.*
I will be driving through the centre of town.
*Anfonwch y siec **trwy**'r post!*
Send the cheque through the post!

Trwy'r amser
All the time
Maen nhw'n siarad Cymraeg â ni trwy'r amser.
They speak Welsh to us all the time.

Trwyn *[eg]*
> trwynau
Nose
Mae trwyn hir gyda fe.
He's got a long nose.

Tu ôl i
Behind
Mae maes parcio mawr tu ôl i'r siop.
There's a big car park behind the shop.

Tudalen *[eb]*
> tudalennau
Page
Roedd gair Cymraeg newydd ar bob tudalen.
There was a new Welsh word on every page.

Twp
Stupid
Roedd y dyn yn dweud llawer o bethau twp.
The man was saying lots of stupid things.

Twym
Hot
Yn Sbaen, mae hi'n dwym iawn ym mis Awst.
In Spain, it's very hot in August.

Tŷ *[eg]*
> tai
House
Dyn ni'n byw mewn tŷ hyfryd yn y wlad.
We live in a lovely house in the country.

Tŷ bach *[eg]*
> tai bach
Toilet [Also: Toiled(au)]
Ble mae'r tŷ bach, os gwelwch yn dda?
Where's the toilet please?

Tywydd *[eg]*
Weather
Sut mae'r tywydd heddiw?
How's the weather today? / What's the weather like today?

TH

Theatr [eb]　　　*Theatre*
> theatrau　　　　*Mae'r actor yn gweithio mewn theatr.*
　　　　　　　　The actor works in a theatre.

U

Uned [eb]　　　*Unit*
> unedau　　　　*Heno, byddwn ni'n edrych ar uned newydd.*
　　　　　　　　Tonight, we will be looking at a new unit.

Unigol* 　　　*Singular*
Unman　　　　*Nowhere / Anywhere*
　　　　　　　　Dw i ddim yn gallu gweld y plant yn unman.
　　　　　　　　I can't see the children anywhere.

Unwaith (eto)　*Once (again)*
　　　　　　　　Da iawn! Unwaith eto, os gwelwch yn dda!
　　　　　　　　Well done! Once again, please!

Ar unwaith　　　*Immediately / Straight away*
　　　　　　　　Dewch i'r ysgol ar unwaith.
　　　　　　　　Come to school immediately.

W

Wal [eb]　　　*Wall*
> waliau　　　　*Bydda i'n rhoi'r llun ar y wal.*
　　　　　　　　I will be putting the picture on the wall.

Wedi　　　　*(i) Past*
　　　　　　　　Mae'n bum munud wedi saith.
　　　　　　　　It's five minutes past seven.

(ii) Way of making the perfect tense in Welsh e.g. **has** *gone rather than* **is** *going.*

Dych chi **wedi** *bwyta eto?*

Have *you* **eaten** *yet?*

Wedyn
(i) After(wards)

Bydda i'n eich gweld chi **wedyn**.

I'll be seeing you **after(wards)**.

(ii) Then (i.e. what happened next)

Wedyn, *aeth pawb i'r dafarn.*

Then, *everyone went to the pub.*

Weithiau
Sometimes

Weithiau, *dw i'n anghofio ei enw fe.*

Sometimes, *I forget his name.*

Wrth
By / At / Beside [See also > **Dweud / Dweud wrth**] *+ Treiglad Meddal*

Pwy sy **wrth** *y drws?*

Who's **at** *the door?*

Maen nhw'n byw i lawr **wrth d***afarn y pentre.*

They live down **by** *the village pub.*

Wrth gwrs
Of course

Dych chi'n siarad Cymraeg? **Wrth gwrs**!

Do you speak Welsh? **Of course**!

Wrth ymyl
Close, near

Mae Stadiwm y Mileniwm **wrth ymyl** *canol Caerdydd.*

The Millennium Stadium is **near** *to the centre of Cardiff.*

[See also > **Agos**]

Wy *[eg]*
> wyau
Egg

Dyn ni'n cael **wy** *a sglodion i de eto heno!*

We're having **egg** *and chips for tea again tonight!*

Wythnos *[eb]*
> wythnosau
Week

Bydd y dosbarth yn dechrau yr **wythnos** *nesa.*

The class will be starting next **week**.

Y

Y / Yr/ 'r	*The*
	*Dw i'n gweld **y** car.*
	*I see **the** car.*
	*Dw i'n gyrru'**r** car.*
	*I drive **the** car.*
	*Car **yr** heddlu yw e.*
	*It's **the** police car – it's **the** car of the police.*
Yfed	*To drink*
	*Dyn ni ddim yn gyrru ar ôl **yfed**.*
	*We don't drive after **drinking**.*
Yfory	*See > **Fory***
Yma	*Here [SW sometimes: **fan hyn**]*
	*Ydy Siân **yma**? / Ydy Siân **fan hyn**?*
	Is Siân here?
Ymarfer*	*To practise*
Ymddeol	*(i) To retire*
	*Bydda i'n **ymddeol** y flwyddyn nesa.*
	*I will be **retiring** next year.*
	(ii) Wedi ymddeol = retired
	*Mae Jac **wedi ymddeol** yn barod.*
	*Jac has already **retired**.*
Ymlacio	*To relax*
	*Dw i'n hoffi **ymlacio** yn y bath ar ôl y dosbarth.*
	*I like to **relax** in the bath after class.*
Ymlaen	*(i) On*
	*Mae'r teledu **ymlaen** trwy'r amser.*
	*The television is **on** all the time.*
	(ii) Ahead / Forward
	*Dw i'n mynd i symud **ymlaen** i'r cwrs Sylfaen.*
	*I'm going to move **on** / **forward** / **ahead** to the Sylfaen course.*

Ymolchi	*To wash (yourself), to have a wash*
	*Bob bore, dw i'n codi ac yn **ymolchi** cyn gwisgo.*
	*Every morning, I get up and **have a wash** before getting dressed.*
Yn	*Not translated in English but used:*
	(i) with a verb-noun
	*Mae Siân **yn** siarad Cymraeg.*
	Siân **speaks / is speaking** *Welsh: yn + siarad.*
	(ii) with an Adjective + Treiglad Meddal
	*Mae'r car **yn g**och.*
	*The car is **red**: yn + coch.*
	(iii) with an adverb + Treiglad Meddal
	*Mae Llinos yn rhedeg **yn g**yflym.*
	*Llinos runs **quickly**: yn + cyflym.*
Yn	*In + Treiglad Trwynol [BUT: In + language + Treiglad Meddal]*
	*Dw i wedi gadael fy llyfr **yn** y car.*
	*I have left my book **in** the car.*
	*Dw i wedi gadael fy llyfr **yng ngh**ar fy ffrind.*
	*I have left my book **in** my friend's car.*
	*Mae'r llyfr **yn G**ymraeg.*
	*The book is **in** Welsh.*
Yn ôl / 'Nôl	*(i) Back*
	*Des i '**nôl** i Gymru i fyw.*
	*I came **back** to Wales to live.*
	(ii) According to
	Yn ôl ein tiwtor, dyn ni'n siarad yn dda!
	According to *our tutor, we speak well!*
Yna	*There [SW sometimes: fan'na]*
	*Does dim byd **yna** / Does dim byd **fan'na**.*
	*There's nothing **there**.*
Yr Alban	*Scotland*
	*Mae Fiona'n dod o Glasgow yn **yr** Alban.*
	*Fiona comes from Glasgow in **Scotland**.*

Yr Eidal　　　*Italy*
　　　　　　　*Dych chi wedi bod ym Milan yn **yr Eidal** erioed?*
　　　　　　　Have you ever been in Milan in Italy?

Ysbyty [eg]　*Hospital*
> ysbytai　　　*Aethon ni i'r **ysbyty** ar ôl y ddamwain.*
　　　　　　　We went to the hospital after the accident.

Ysgol [eb]　　*School*
> ysgolion　　*Bydd fy mhlentyn yn dechrau yn yr **ysgol** y mis nesa.*
　　　　　　　My child will be starting in school next month.

Ysgrifennu (at) *To write (to a person):* [Also: **Sgrifennu / Sgwennu**]
　　　　　　　*Dw i'n mynd i **ysgrifennu** llythyr.*
　　　　　　　I'm going to write a letter.
　　　　　　　*Dw i'n mynd i **ysgrifennu** llythyr **at** fy merch.*
　　　　　　　I'm going to write a letter to my daughter / I'm going to write my daughter a letter.

Ysgrifenedig*　*Written, in writing*

Ysgrifenyddes [eb] *Secretary [female]*
> ysgrifenyddesau *Mae hi'n gweithio fel **ysgrifenyddes** yn yr ysgol newydd.*
　　　　　　　She's working as a secretary in the new school.

Ysgrifennydd [eg] *Secretary [male]*
> ysgrifenyddion *Mae e'n gweithio fel **ysgrifennydd** yn yr ysgol newydd.*
　　　　　　　He's working as a secretary in the new school.

Ysmygu　　　*[See > **Smygu**]*
Ystafell　　*[See > **Stafell**]*

NUMBERS 1 – 100 and 1,000

1	Un Un **d**rws Un **g**adair
2	Dau / Dwy Dau **dd**rws Dwy **g**adair
3	Tri / Tair Tri **d**rws Tair **c**adair
4	Pedwar / Pedair Pedwar **d**rws Pedair **c**adair
5	Pum[p] Pum **d**rws Pum **c**adair
6	Chwe[ch] Chwe **d**rws Chwe **c**adair / Chwe **ch**adair
7	Saith Saith **d**rws Saith **c**adair
8	Wyth Wyth **d**rws Wyth **c**adair
9	Naw Naw **d**rws Naw **c**adair
10	Deg Deg **d**rws Deg **c**adair
11	Un deg un > Un ar ddeg *[when telling the time]* *Mae'n **un ar ddeg** o'r gloch* = 11:00
12	Un deg dau / dwy > Deuddeg *[when telling the time]* *Mae'n **ddeuddeg** o'r gloch* = 12:00
13	Un deg tri / tair
14	Un deg pedwar / pedair
15	Un deg pump
16	Un deg chwech
17	Un deg saith
18	Un deg wyth
19	Un deg naw
20	Dau ddeg > Ugain munud *[when telling the time]* *Mae'n **ugain** munud wedi wyth* = 08:20 *Mae'n **ugain** munud i bedwar* = 03:40
21	Dau ddeg un
22	Dau ddeg dau / dwy
23	Dau ddeg tri / tair

24	Dau ddeg pedwar / pedair
25	Dau ddeg pump > Pum munud ar hugain

[when telling the time]

Mae'n **bum munud ar hugain** *wedi dau yn y prynhawn = 14:25*

Mae'n **bum munud ar hugain** *i bump yn y prynhawn = 16:35*

26	Dau ddeg chwech
27	Dau ddeg saith
28	Dau ddeg wyth
29	Dau ddeg naw
30	Tri deg
31	Tri deg un
32	Tri deg dau / dwy
33	Tri deg tri / tair
34	Tri deg pedwar / pedair
35	Tri deg pump
36	Tri deg chwech
37	Tri deg saith
38	Tri deg wyth
39	Tri deg naw
40	Pedwar deg
41	Pedwar deg un
42	Pedwar deg dau / dwy
43	Pedwar deg tri / tair
44	Pedwar deg pedwar / pedair
45	Pedwar deg pump
46	Pedwar deg chwech
47	Pedwar deg saith
48	Pedwar deg wyth
49	Pedwar deg naw
50	Pum deg
51	Pum deg un
52	Pum deg dau / dwy

53	Pum deg tri / tair
54	Pum deg pedwar / pedair
55	Pum deg pump
56	Pum deg chwech
57	Pum deg saith
58	Pum deg wyth
59	Pum deg naw
60	Chwe deg
61	Chwe deg un
62	Chwe deg dau / dwy
63	Chwe deg tri / tair
64	Chwe deg pedwar / pedair
65	Chwe deg pump
66	Chwe deg chwech
67	Chwe deg saith
68	Chwe deg wyth
69	Chwe deg naw
70	Saith deg
71	Saith deg un
72	Saith deg dau / dwy
73	Saith deg tri / tair
74	Saith deg pedwar / pedair
75	Saith deg pump
76	Saith deg chwech
77	Saith deg saith
78	Saith deg wyth
79	Saith deg naw
80	Wyth deg
81	Wyth deg un
82	Wyth deg dau / dwy
83	Wyth deg tri / tair
84	Wyth deg pedwar / pedair
85	Wyth deg pump
86	Wyth deg chwech

87	Wyth deg saith
88	Wyth deg wyth
89	Wyth deg naw
90	Naw deg
91	Naw deg un
92	Naw deg dau / dwy
93	Naw deg tri / tair
94	Naw deg pedwar / pedair
95	Naw deg pump
96	Naw deg chwech
97	Naw deg saith
98	Naw deg wyth
99	Naw deg naw
100	Cant
1,000	Mil

1af /Cynta	*1st*
	Dyma'r cwestiwn **cynta** */ Dyma'r uned* **gynta**.
	*This is the **first** question / This is the **first** unit.*
2il / Ail	*2nd* + *Treiglad Meddal*
	Dyma'r **ail** *gwestiwn / Dyma'r* **ail** *uned.*
	*This is the **second** question / This is the **second** unit.*
3ydd / Trydydd	*3rd* + *masculine nouns*
	Dyma'r **trydydd** *cwestiwn.*
	*This is the **third** question.*
3edd / Trydedd	*3rd* + *feminine nouns* + **Treiglad Meddal**
	Dyma'r **drydedd** *uned.*
	*This is the **third** unit.*

HOW TO LEARN A VOCABULARY

L ANGUAGE COURSES often give the impression that you can speak a language by learning a few simple expressions and a few handfuls of words. If all you want to do is buy a cup of coffee or a bus ticket, then this is probably true. But if, like most people, you lead a life which is not entirely predictable, you will soon meet situations where you need a much bigger vocabulary than the words you have been taught in class. Everyday language in Welsh uses thousands of words, but many of these words are not used very often. This means that you need to have two main strategies to be able to cope with the Welsh you will meet outside your classroom. The first strategy is that you need to know the 2,000 or so most frequent words in Welsh, to be able to recognise them instantly, and to be able to use them fluently. Knowing these words means that you will be able to recognise about 80% of all the words you will come across on a regular basis. This is a good start, but to be a fluent performer in Welsh, 2,000 words is only the beginning. If you want to become really fluent then you need to develop a much bigger vocabulary – 10,000 or more.

Ten thousand words is a lot, and you cannot expect your teacher to teach them to you. When you go to a Welsh class, you will perhaps learn ten new words in an hour, so in a ten-week evening class, two hours a week, you can expect to pick up about 200 new words, if you are lucky. Unfortunately, most people forget about half of the new words they learn in class, so your total vocabulary uptake from a class of this sort might be as little as a hundred new words. Obviously, we have a problem here: if you need to develop a large vocabulary, then it's not reasonable to expect to learn them all in class. There are just too many words to learn, and your teacher doesn't have the time to teach them all individually. This means that you need to develop techniques that will help you take charge of your own word learning, and build up your vocabulary outside of your Welsh classes. Successful language learners have always used these techniques, and if you are serious about learning Welsh, then you should learn how to use them too.

These notes discuss ten methods that are generally reckoned to be successful ways of learning words. You might find that the techniques don't all work for you. This is because not all learners are alike: some learners work best with written input, some learners work best with spoken input; some learners can't wait to try out new words they have learned, while others are not confident about using their language in public and prefer to work in private; some learners read a lot while others hardly ever pick up a book. Whatever kind of learner you are, some of the techniques in this article will work for you. When you find the ones that work, develop them for yourself. Remember, when it comes to learning vocabulary, the only person who can do it is you.

1 Set your self a daily target

The first thing you need to do to take charge of your vocabulary learning is to set yourself a daily target. It doesn't really matter what this target is, though it needs to be a realistic one. For most people, it's NOT realistic to set a target of 50 words a day. On the other hand, a target of one word a day IS realistic, but isn't going to get you very far. So set yourself a target of two or three words a day: this is enough to be challenging, and if you keep it up then you will have learned nearly a thousand words in a year. The trick is to be absolutely systematic about this: do it every day, including weekends and holidays. Learning new words needs to become part of your daily routine, like brushing your teeth.

This method is particularly important for beginners. This book will provide you with some particularly important words which occur frequently in everyday Welsh.

2 Learn to use a Memory System

It's almost impossible to learn new words just by looking at lists in a book. Serious language learners use a memory system. Some people claim that they can learn hundreds of words in a few hours using these systems, but it's much better to learn a few words at a time. Memory systems are particularly useful for beginners, who can greatly benefit from developing their vocabulary at a very fast rate.

The best memory system is the linkword method. At first sight, this method looks a bit complicated, but it really does work. Here is what you have to do to use this method.

Suppose you want to learn the word *ci*, meaning *dog*. First, find an English word that sounds a bit like *ci*. A good one to use would be KEY, which sounds almost exactly like *ci*. Next, make up a picture which involves a DOG and a KEY. For example, you might think of a clockwork DOG with a large KEY sticking out of its back, or you might think of a DOG carrying a large KEY in its mouth, or a DOG burying a big KEY instead of a bone. Basically, any image that links DOG and KEY will work, but in general funny images, or bizarre ones, work best. Think about this image for a few seconds. What you are doing here is building a chain of connections between *ci* and DOG, with KEY forming a link between them, like this:

ci   KEY   dog

It's very easy to remember that *ci* and KEY go together because they both sound the same. It's also easy to remember KEY and DOG, because we have created a funny image involving a dog doing something odd with a key. This creates an almost automatic link between *ci* and *DOG*.

The reason the linkword method works is because it helps you remember the shape of the words that you are trying to learn. If you think of a word as consisting of two parts, a FORM and a MEANING, most people think that the hard part about learning words is remembering which MEANING goes with a particular FORM. In fact, the really hard thing about learning new words is remembering the FORM long enough for a MEANING to become attached to it. The linkword method makes the FORMS easier to remember. It takes a bit of extra effort, but after a while you will find that you don't need the linkword any more: you just have a direct connection between *ci* and *dog*.

It's not always easy to find keywords for Welsh words, because the shape of Welsh words is very different from the shape of English words. Your linkword doesn't have to be a complete match to the Welsh word you are trying to learn – often just a part of the word will do.

Sometimes, you can find a linkword that doesn't rely on a visual image. For example, if you are trying to learn *telyn* (meaning *harp*), then you might decide that *telyn* sounds a bit like TELL LYNNE, and you could make up a short sentence like *Tell Lynne about the harp* to help you remember *telyn,* like this:

telyn   Tell Lynne about the harp   harp

Some people find these verbal images much more effective than visual ones. Work out which one works best for you.

3 Watch out for 'free' words

Although Welsh vocabulary looks very hard at first sight, there are actually a lot of 'free' words in Welsh that you will know already, and other 'almost free' words that are easy to recognise once your vocabulary starts to grow. Over the years, Welsh has borrowed lots of words from English, and they are very easy to recognise. Welsh has also adopted a lot of words which might be familiar to you in other languages: *ffenest* (window) is a bit like *fenêtre* in French – both of them come from the Latin word for window; *eglwys* (church) sounds a bit like French *église* – they both come from the Latin word for church *ecclesia,* which also pops up in the English word *ecclesiastical; ceffyl* (horse) looks a bit like the French word *cheval* – they both come from the Latin word for horse; *cadair* (chair) is related to the English word *cathedral* – a church where a bishop's *throne* is located.

Difficult-looking Welsh words are often made up from smaller easier ones, and you should try to recognise these small words in the new words you are learning. *Llyfrgell* (library) is made up of *llyfr* (book) and *cell* (store); *llawlyfr* (a manual) is made up from *llaw* (hand) and *llyfr* (book); *mewnfudiad* (immigration) is made up from *mewn* (in) and *mudiad* (movement). Welsh has lots of words like this, and it will greatly help you if can learn to recognise them.

There are also some systematic correspondences between the beginnings of Welsh words and the beginnings of English words. Words that begin with AIL- are often related to English words that begin with RE- (*ailagor* – ail + agor = reopen; *ailfeddwl* – ail + meddwl = rethink). Words that begin with CYD- are often related to English words that start with CO- (*cydweithio* – cyd +

gweithio = cooperate). Words that begin with CAM- often relate to English words beginning with MIS- (*cam-drin* – cam + trin = mistreat; *camarwain* – cam + arwain = mislead). If you keep an eye out for correspondences of this sort, you will significantly reduce your learning load, particularly for less usual words.

4 Learn new words in context

Learning new words in a context is a lot easier than trying to learn lists of words and their meanings. A good way to do this is to use headlines from magazines. Headlines are usually quite short, and they carry a lot of information. For example, a word like *ystyried* (consider) is quite difficult to learn on its own, but in a context like: *Ystyried codi trydedd bont dros y Fenai* (Consider building a third bridge across the Menai Strait) is much easier to remember. If you buy a copy of the Welsh weekly magazine *Golwg*, then you will find lots of examples of this sort. These headlines come with the added advantage of being fairly topical, and this means that they may contain words that you are likely to meet in other contexts, such as listening to the Welsh-language news on S4C.

A good way to work with headline contexts is to find a headline that contains a word you don't know. Look up the meaning of the unknown word in a dictionary, and write the headline out on a small card. On the back of the card write the unknown word. Keep a stack of these cards somewhere handy. Then once a day work through your stack of cards. Look at the back of the card and try to recall the meaning of the word. If you don't know it, turn the card over, and the context should be enough to jog your memory. Doing this ten times should fix the word in your memory without too much extra effort.

5 Read something every day

The only reliable way to build up a very large vocabulary quickly is by reading, and you should make a point of reading something every day. Be sensible about what you choose to read. Heavy literature and serious novels are not a good idea for beginners – no one can read a story if they have to look up two or three words in each line in a dictionary. In any case, works of this kind will contain lots of words that aren't useful for you. A good thing to read is a storybook aimed at young children: the story lines in these texts will usually be predictable and easy to understand, and there are usually lots of pictures in books of this sort, which will help you to guess the meanings of words you don't know. Storybooks for children usually have a lot of repetition in them too, and repetition increases your chances of learning new words. The more often a word appears in what you read, the more likely you are to learn it, so don't be embarrassed by reading books that seem really simple and childish. They WILL help you acquire a basic vocabulary. And don't be afraid to read the same book several times.

For beginners, audiobooks are a useful way to read. Listen to the story at the same time as you read the words on the page.

If you are able to read slightly more advanced stories, where there is more text and fewer pictures, then there is a good trick that you can do to convince yourself that your vocabulary is getting bigger. Find a story which you can just about read with the help of a dictionary. Start reading, and keep going until you have had to look up ten words, then stop. Count how many lines of text you read, and keep a record of this figure. Next day, read what you read yesterday (this will rehearse the new words you learned yesterday, and remind you of what the story is about). Then read on until you have found another ten words that you had to look up. Count the number of lines you read before you reached ten new words. You should find that you can gradually extend the number of lines you can read before you meet the ten-word threshold.

Another good idea with reading is to take a text that you know well in English and find a translation in Welsh. Then read a couple of paragraphs in English, and read the same couple of paragraphs in the Welsh translation. The fact that you already know what the Welsh text means will make it easy for you to 'understand' the Welsh, and to guess the meanings of any words that you don't know.

6 Write something every day

When you learn new words, it's a good idea to use them as soon as possible. There are two ways to do this. One is to engineer a situation where you can use the word in a natural context. For example if you learn the word for carrots (*moron*), make a point of going to buy carrots at your local friendly Welsh-speaking greengrocer's shop as soon as possible. If this isn't possible, then the best thing you can do is just write this word down in a short sentence. As with reading, it's a good idea to keep a list of 'writing words'. Write your new word on the back of a small card, and write a phrase or a short sentence that contains this word on the front. When you have a stack of these cards, you can work through them one at a time, reviewing the sentences you already wrote, and adding a new sentence on each card. By the time you have done this five or six times over the course of a few days, you should have learnt the new words.

7 Listen to songs

There is a lot of evidence that words you learn in musical contexts are much better learned than words that you only meet in speech. Some psychologists think that this is because musical input is processed deep inside your brain, whereas ordinary speech is processed in a shallower way. Either way, there is a lot of evidence that people are much more likely to remember songs than they are to remember ordinary speech, and even when you forget your first language, you are often able to remember things like nursery rhymes and chants that you knew in childhood. Songs with good lyrics often have a chorus which repeats some of the main words in the lyrics, and this provides an added support. What you need to do here is listen to the same songs over and over until you know them off by heart, and can sing along with the artist. You can start by listening and reading the lyrics, but after a while, you should find that you can manage without the written lyrics.

Some people think that you can learn vocabulary more effectively if you study word lists while you listen to instrumental music, especially if you do this just before you go to bed. New Age soft background music is supposed to be very good, but the actual evidence on the effectiveness of this method is not very strong. My own view on this idea is that what makes it work is the ritual aspect of sitting down and playing a particular piece of calming music. Sitting down in the same place, with the same music, at the same time of day creates a sort of psychological space and lets you focus on the vocabulary learning task more consciously than you would otherwise.

8 Make your vocabulary fluent

Another way to practise your vocabulary is to buy a set of picture postcards, preferably postcards of a place you are familiar with. Take ten of the postcards and put them in a pile. Take each postcard, and find five things that you can name or describe. Time how long it takes you to complete this task for all ten postcards. You should find that the completion time goes down steadily if you do this task once a week. After a while, however, the completion time will level out and stop getting shorter. When that happens you should increase the number of words you find for each card. When you can generate ten words for each postcard without hesitating, stop counting the words you know really well and find a more difficult word. For example, if your postcard is a picture of Barry Island in summer, you might decide that *mam* (mum) and *plant* (children) or *môr* (sea) are too easy, and try other words instead. Alternatively, you could start to look for two-word phrases instead of single words (*mam hapus*, or *plant bach*). If you do this task regularly, you will find that you start noticing new words that you could use with your postcards, and this will make it easier for you to learn them.

The idea here is that repeating this task will show you how much better you are getting, and how much more fluent your use of Welsh words is becoming.

9 Watch DVDs with subtitles

A really good way of increasing your vocabulary is to watch DVDs and TV programmes that use subtitles. There are two ways of doing this. One is to watch Welsh-language programmes with English subtitles. This will help you understand what you are listening to. Even if you cannot catch exactly what words are being used, you will understand what is being said, and this will make it more likely that you will catch the words another time. This idea works particularly well if you can watch the same programme several times over – you can do this if you get hold of some Welsh-language films which come with English subtitles. The other way to use subtitles is to watch Welsh-language TV programmes with subtitles in Welsh provided for people who are hard of hearing. This has the advantage that you can actually see the words that are being spoken. Same language subtitles make it very much easier to catch what is being said, and will help you recognise new words more quickly. If you have a CD-ROM with Welsh-language subtitles, then you can try turning the sound down and reading the subtitles out loud. You have to be pretty quick to do this, as the subtitles remain on screen for a fairly short time. Again, this works best if you watch a film that you are already familiar with. Keep track of how many subtitles you can read out loud before they disappear. You should find that the number goes up each time you do this task.

10 Use your local resources

In most localities in Wales there is lots of Welsh on the street. Make sure that you can read and understand any notices in your area. Make sure that you can translate your local street names. If you live in a strongly Welsh-speaking area you will find that lots of houses where you live will have Welsh names – make sure that you understand all the ones in the streets near you.

The ten techniques that I have outlined here will provide you with a set of simple tools for picking up new words and making them part of your own vocabulary. The key message here is **do it yourself!** Your teacher will only be able to teach you a few words in class, and you need to take charge of your own learning if you want to become really proficient in Welsh. It's particularly important to build up a large vocabulary incrementally, learning a few words every day over a very long time.

The ten techniques I have outlined above are all standard ideas with a lot of research to back them up. However, there is another method which I have found useful that you might be able to use for yourself. I call it the Fahrenheit 451 method, after Ray Bradbury's novel of the same name. In Bradbury's novel, society has decided that books are a bad thing, and crews of firemen track down illicit collections of books and burn them. A few people on the edge of society have decided that they must preserve these books, and they each undertake to learn a book off by heart, so that they can pass it on even when the physical texts have been destroyed. The Fahrenheit 451 method uses the same idea. It suggests that a good way to learn a very large advanced vocabulary in a foreign language is to learn a long text off by heart.

This idea is not a new one, of course. It was used a lot by nineteenth-century missionaries who would often learn new languages by memorising large parts of the Bible in the language of the country they were working in. The fact that they were very highly motivated, and the fact that they were already familiar with the English texts made it fairly simple to learn very long foreign language texts in this way, and provided the missionaries with a large vocabulary which was highly relevant to their work. The Gospel of St Mark, for example, the shortest of the four Gospels, and very familiar to any missionary, contains about 13,000 running words. If you learned that text off by heart – or even fairly well – then you would end up with a vocabulary of around 5,000 different words, and have no trouble learning what they mean and how to use them.

Learning texts off by heart is not a method that curries much favour in modern language teaching methods, but I think it might be due for a re-evaluation. The problem is that we don't have any modern texts that act as a shared reference point, as the Bible did in the nineteenth century, or the Communist Manifesto did in the twentieth century. However, if you can find a Welsh translation of a book that is particularly important to you, then give this method a try. Even a short book – one that you could read comfortably in a couple of hours – will give you a vocabulary of several thousand words.

Paul Meara

July 2014

Hefyd ar gael o'r Lolfa:

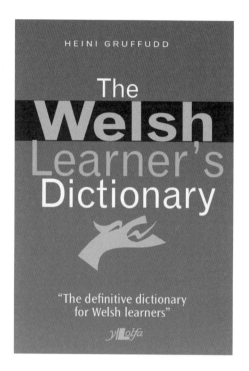

THE WELSH LEARNER'S DICTIONARY
Y geiriadur hanfodol i ddysgwyr.
The essential Welsh learner's dictionary.
0 86243 363 0
£6.95

WELSH IN YOUR POCKET
Hanfodion yr iaith ar gardiau consertina!
Learn Welsh on the go: it's all on a couple of concertina cards!
9 781 84771 877 8
£3.95